# Accumula 5

## STUDENT BOOK

**JUMP Math**
One Yonge Street, Suite 1014
Toronto, Ontario M5E 1E5
Canada
www.jumpmath.org

Writers: Dr. John Mighton, Dr. Anna Klebanov, Dr. Sohrab Rahbar, Saverio Mercurio
Consultant: Dr. Sindi Sabourin
Editors: Dishpreet Kaur, Dimitra Chronopoulos, Laura Edlund, Ewa Krynski
Layout and Illustrations: Linh Lam, Gabriella Kerr
Cover Design: Sunday Lek
Cover Photograph: © vecstock/Freepik.com

ISBN 978-1-77395-297-0

First printing January 2024

Parts of this material were first published in 2013 in AP Book 5.1, US edition (978-1-927457-14-6) and AP Book 5.2, US edition (978-1-927457-15-3).

Printed and bound in Canada

# Welcome to JUMP Math!

Entering the world of JUMP Math means believing that every learner has the capacity to be fully numerate and love math.

The **JUMP Math Accumula Student Book** is the companion to the **JUMP Math Accumula** supplementary resource for Grades 1 to 8, which is designed to strengthen foundational math knowledge and prepare all students for success in understanding math problems at grade level. This book provides opportunities for students to consolidate learning by exploring important math concepts through independent practice.

## Unique Evidence-Based Approach and Resources

JUMP Math's unique approach, Kindergarten to Grade 8 resources, and professional learning for teachers have been producing positive learning outcomes for children and teachers in classrooms in Canada, the United States, and other countries for over 20 years. Our resources are aligned with the science on how children's brains learn best and have been demonstrated through studies to greatly improve problem solving, computation, and fluency skills. (See our research at **jumpmath.org**.) Our approach is designed to build equity by supporting the full spectrum of learners to achieve success in math.

## Confidence Building is Key

JUMP Math begins each grade with review to enable every student to quickly develop the confidence needed to engage deeply with math. Our distinctive incremental approach to learning math concepts gradually increases the level of difficulty for students, empowering them to become motivated, independent problem solvers. Our books are also designed with simple pictures and models to avoid overwhelming learners when introducing new concepts, enabling them to see the deep structure of the math and gain the confidence to solve a wide range of math problems.

## About JUMP Math

JUMP Math is a non-profit organization dedicated to helping every child in every classroom develop confidence, understanding, and a love of math. JUMP Math also offers a comprehensive set of classroom resources for students in Kindergarten to Grade 8.

**For more information, visit JUMP Math at: www.jumpmath.org.**

# Contents

# 1. Introduction to Multiplication

Multiplication is repeated addition.

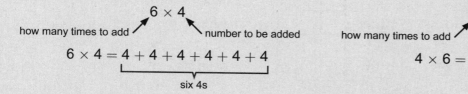

$6 \times 4$
how many times to add — number to be added

$6 \times 4 = 4 + 4 + 4 + 4 + 4 + 4$
six 4s

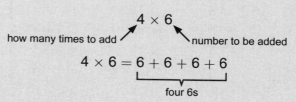

$4 \times 6$
how many times to add — number to be added

$4 \times 6 = 6 + 6 + 6 + 6$
four 6s

Michela noticed that $4 + 4 + 4 + 4 + 4 + 4 = 24$ and $6 + 6 + 6 + 6 = 24$

**So $6 \times 4 = 4 \times 6$. This is an example of the commutative property.**

1. Write the multiplication statement as repeated addition.

   a) $5 \times 3 = $ _____ $3 + 3 + 3 + 3 + 3$ _____

   b) $6 \times 7 = $ _____

   c) $4 \times 9 = $ _____

   d) $3 \times 9 = $ _____

   e) $2 \times 8 = $ _____

   f) $7 \times 1 = $ _____

   **BONUS ▶**

   g) $4 \times 748 = $ _____

   h) $3 \times 1,285 = $ _____

2. Write the repeated addition as a multiplication statement.

   a) $7 + 7 + 7 + 7 = $ _____ $4 \times 7$ _____

   b) $9 + 9 + 9 = $ _____

   c) $6 + 6 + 6 + 6 + 6 = $ _____

   d) $2 + 2 + 2 + 2 + 2 + 2 + 2 = $ _____

   e) $8 + 8 = $ _____

   f) $1 + 1 + 1 + 1 + 1 + 1 + 1 + 1 + 1 = $ _____

3. Calculate the product.

   a) $5 \times 4 = $ _____ $4 + 4 + 4 + 4 + 4$ _____ $= $ __ $20$ __

   b) $4 \times 5 = $ _____ $= $ _____

   c) $6 \times 2 = $ _____ $= $ _____

   d) $2 \times 6 = $ _____ $= $ _____

   e) $7 \times 1 = $ _____ $= $ _____

   f) $1 \times 7 = $ _____ $= $ _____

   g) $8 \times 3 = $ _____ $= $ _____

   h) $3 \times 8 = $ _____ $= $ _____

4. Fill in the blanks to complete the equation.

   a) $9 \times 8 = 72$  so  __ $8$ __ $\times$ __ $9$ __ $= $ __ $72$ __

   b) $5 \times 3 = 15$  so  ____ $\times$ ____ $= $ _____

   c) $4 \times 8 = 32$  so  ____ $\times$ ____ $= $ _____

   d) $6 \times 7 = 42$  so  ____ $\times$ ____ $= $ _____

   e) $8 \times 7 = 56$  so  ____ $\times$ ____ $= $ _____

   f) $4 \times 9 = 36$  so  ____ $\times$ ____ $= $ _____

   **BONUS ▶** $245 \times 983 = 240,835$  so  _____ $\times$ _____ $= $ _____

An **array** is a picture that shows multiplication:

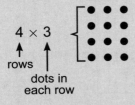

$4 \times 3$

↑ rows

↑ dots in each row

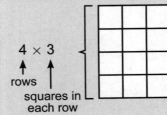

$4 \times 3$

↑ rows

↑ squares in each row

**5.** Write a product for the array.

a)  $\underline{4 \times 2}$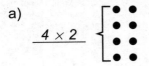

b)  _____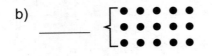

c)  _____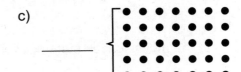

d)  _____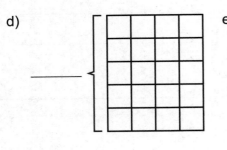

e)  _____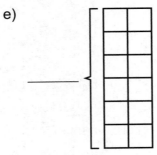

f)  _____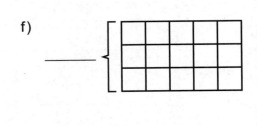

**6.** Write a product for the array.

a)  _____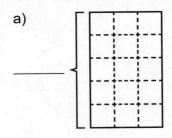

b)  _____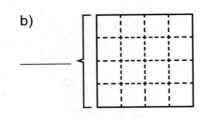

c)  _____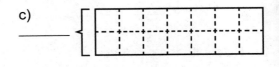

**7.** Write a product for the array.

a)  _____ × _____

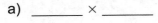

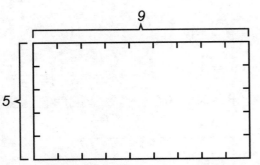

b)  _____ × _____

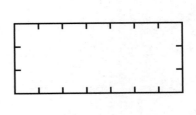

# 2. Multiplication by Adding On

Ava knows how to find $5 \times 4$ by adding five 4s ($4 + 4 + 4 + 4 + 4 = 20$). Her teacher asks her how she can find $6 \times 4$ without adding six 4s.

Ava knows that $6 \times 4$ is one more 4 than $5 \times 4$. She shows this in three ways:

**With a picture using dots**

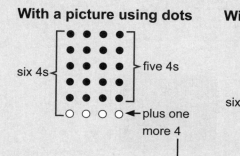

**With a picture using squares**

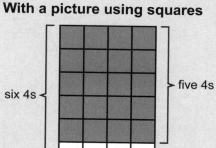

**By adding**

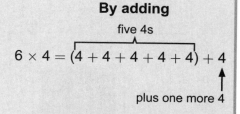

$$6 \times 4 = (4 + 4 + 4 + 4 + 4) + 4$$

Ava knows that $6 \times 4 = (5 \times 4) + 4$.

She knows $5 \times 4 = 20$, so $6 \times 4 = 20 + 4 = 24$.

**1.** Fill in the missing product and the added number.

a) $\underline{\ 4 \times 6\ }$  $\underline{\ 3 \times 6\ }$

$+\ \underline{\ 6\ }$

b) $\underline{\quad\quad}$ $\underline{\quad\quad}$

$+\underline{\quad\quad}$

c) $\underline{\quad\quad}$ $\underline{\quad\quad}$

$+\underline{\quad\quad}$

d) $\underline{\quad\quad}$ $\underline{\quad\quad}$

$+\underline{\quad\quad}$

e) $\underline{\quad\quad}$ 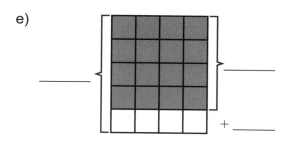 $\underline{\quad\quad}$

$+\underline{\quad\quad}$

f) $\underline{\quad\quad}$ 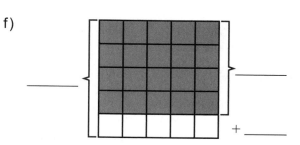 $\underline{\quad\quad}$

$+\underline{\quad\quad}$

g) $\underline{\quad\quad}$ 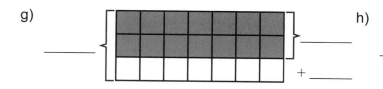 $\underline{\quad\quad}$

$+\underline{\quad\quad}$

h) $\underline{\quad\quad}$ 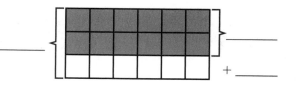 $\underline{\quad\quad}$

$+\underline{\quad\quad}$

**2.** Fill in the missing product and the added number. Then write the equation.

a)

$4 \times 6$ { [dots] } $3 \times 6$
$+\underline{\phantom{6}6\phantom{6}}$

$\underline{\phantom{xxxx}4 \times 6 = (3 \times 6) + 6\phantom{xxxx}}$

b)

$\underline{\phantom{xxx}}$ { [dots] } $\underline{\phantom{xxx}}$
$+\underline{\phantom{xxx}}$

$\underline{\phantom{xxxxxxxxxxxxxxxxxxxxxxxxxxxxxxxxxx}}$

c)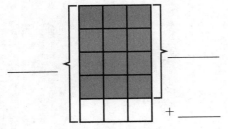

$\underline{\phantom{xxx}}$ { [grid] } $\underline{\phantom{xxx}}$
$+\underline{\phantom{xxx}}$

$\underline{\phantom{xxxxxxxxxxxxxxxxxxx}}$

d)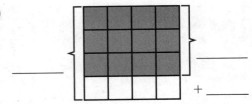

$\underline{\phantom{xxx}}$ { [grid] } $\underline{\phantom{xxx}}$
$+\underline{\phantom{xxx}}$

$\underline{\phantom{xxxxxxxxxxxxxxxxxxx}}$

---

You can always turn a product into a smaller product and a sum.

$5 \times 7 = (\mathbf{4} \times 7) + \mathbf{7}$

take 1 away from 5     add an extra 7

$9 \times 3 = (\mathbf{8} \times 3) + \mathbf{3}$

take 1 away from 9     add an extra 3

---

**3.** Turn the product into a smaller product and a sum.

a) $4 \times 6 = (3 \times \underline{\phantom{x}6\phantom{x}}) + \underline{\phantom{x}6\phantom{x}}$

b) $4 \times 7 = (3 \times \underline{\phantom{xxx}}) + \underline{\phantom{xxx}}$

c) $8 \times 5 = (7 \times \underline{\phantom{xxx}}) + \underline{\phantom{xxx}}$

d) $6 \times 6 = (5 \times \underline{\phantom{xxx}}) + \underline{\phantom{xxx}}$

e) $7 \times 3 = (\underline{\phantom{xxx}} \times \underline{\phantom{xxx}}) + \underline{\phantom{xxx}}$

f) $8 \times 7 = (\underline{\phantom{xxx}} \times \underline{\phantom{xxx}}) + \underline{\phantom{xxx}}$

g) $8 \times 6 = \underline{\phantom{xxxxxxxxxxxxxxxxx}}$

h) $9 \times 4 = \underline{\phantom{xxxxxxxxxxxxxxxxx}}$

**4.** Find the answer by turning the product into a smaller product and a sum.

a) $5 \times 8 = \underline{\phantom{xxxx}(4 \times 8) + 8\phantom{xxxx}}$

$= \underline{\phantom{xxx}32 + 8\phantom{xxx}}$

$= \underline{\phantom{xxx}40\phantom{xxx}}$

b) $6 \times 4 = \underline{\phantom{xxxxxxxxxxxxxxx}}$

$= \underline{\phantom{xxxxxxxxxxxxxxx}}$

$= \underline{\phantom{xxxxx}}$

c) $9 \times 6 = \underline{\phantom{xxxxxxxxxxxxxxx}}$

$= \underline{\phantom{xxxxxxxxxxxxxxx}}$

$= \underline{\phantom{xxxxx}}$

d) $7 \times 5 = \underline{\phantom{xxxxxxxxxxxxxxx}}$

$= \underline{\phantom{xxxxxxxxxxxxxxx}}$

$= \underline{\phantom{xxxxx}}$

# 3. Multiplying by Tens, Hundreds, and Thousands

To multiply 2 × 30, Chris makes 2 groups of 3 tens blocks (30 = 3 tens).

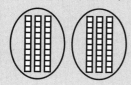

2 × 30 = 2 × 3 tens = 6 tens = 60

To multiply 2 × 300, Chris makes 2 groups of 3 hundreds blocks (300 = 3 hundreds).

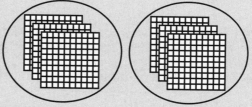

2 × 300 = 2 × 3 hundreds = 6 hundreds = 600

Chris notices a pattern:     2 × 3 = 6     2 × 30 = 60     2 × 300 = 600

1. Draw a model for the multiplication statement. Then calculate the answer.

a) 2 × 40                               b) 3 × 30

   2 × 40 = 2 × _____ tens = _____ tens = _____          3 × 30 = 3 × _____ tens = _____ tens = _____

2. Regroup to find the answer.

a) 3 × 70 = 3 × ___7___ tens = ___21___ tens = ___210___

b) 4 × 60 = 4 × _____ tens = _____ tens = _____

c) 5 × 70 = 5 × _____ tens = _____ tens = _____

d) 8 × 40 = 8 × _____ tens = _____ tens = _____

3. Fill in the answer to complete the pattern.

a) 3 × 2 = _____       b) 7 × 1 = _____       c) 2 × 4 = _____       d) 7 × 2 = _____

   3 × 20 = _____         7 × 10 = _____         2 × 40 = _____         7 × 20 = _____

   3 × 200 = _____        7 × 100 = _____        2 × 400 = _____        7 × 200 = _____

4. Multiply.

a) 4 × 20 = _____       b) 3 × 30 = _____       c) 2 × 40 = _____       d) 3 × 50 = _____

e) 7 × 100 = _____      f) 2 × 300 = _____      g) 3 × 400 = _____      h) 6 × 200 = _____

i) 5 × 70 = _____       j) 4 × 60 = _____       k) 9 × 20 = _____       l) 8 × 300 = _____

5. Draw a base ten model to show 3 × 2,000. Use a cube to represent a thousand.

6. You know that 4 × 2 = 8. How can you use this fact to multiply 4 × 2,000?

$10 \times \square = $ |      $10 \times$ | $= \square$     $10 \times \square = $ ▱

10 × 1 one = 1 ten     10 × 1 ten = 1 hundred     10 × 1 hundred = 1 thousand

**7.** Draw a model for the multiplication statement. Then calculate the answer.

a) $10 \times 20 = 10 \times$ ||| $= \square\ \square$      $= \underline{\quad 200 \quad}$

b) $10 \times 300 = 10 \times \square\ \square\ \square = $ ▱ ▱ ▱      $= \underline{\qquad}$

c) $10 \times 30 = 10 \times$ |||| $= $      $= \underline{\qquad}$

d) $10 \times 4 = 10 \times \square\square\square\square = $      $= \underline{\qquad}$

e) $10 \times 40 = 10 \times$      $= \underline{\qquad}$

f) $10 \times 200 = $      $= \underline{\qquad}$

**8.** Multiply.

a) $10 \times 5 = \underline{\qquad}$     b) $10 \times 60 = \underline{\qquad}$     c) $10 \times 30 = \underline{\qquad}$

d) $10 \times 200 = \underline{\qquad}$     e) $10 \times 8 = \underline{\qquad}$     f) $10 \times 400 = \underline{\qquad}$

**BONUS** ▶ $10 \times 30{,}000{,}000 = \underline{\qquad\qquad\qquad\qquad}$

To multiply 20 × 60, Shahira multiplies (2 × 10) × (6 × 10).

A 20 × 60 rectangle can be divided into 12 rectangles of 10 × 10 each. Shahira multiplies:

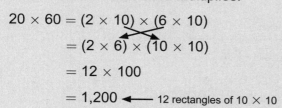

20 × 60 = (2 × 10) × (6 × 10)

    = (2 × 6) × (10 × 10)

    = 12 × 100

    = 1,200 ◀——— 12 rectangles of 10 × 10

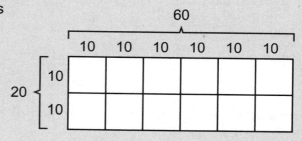

9. Multiply.

a) 30 × 40 = (3 × 10) × (4 × 10)

    = (3 × 4) × (10 × 10)

    = 12 × ____100____

    = ____1,200____

b) 20 × 70 = (2 × 10) × (7 × 10)

    = (2 × 7) × (10 × 10)

    = _____ × _____

    = _____

c) 20 × 400 = (2 × 10) × (4 × 100)

    = (2 × 4) × (10 × 100)

    = 8 × ____1,000____

    = ____8,000____

d) 40 × 400 = (4 × 10) × (4 × 100)

    = (4 × 4) × (10 × 100)

    = _____ × _____

    = _____

Follow the steps to multiply 40 × 700:

**Step 1:** Multiply 4 × 7 = 28

**Step 2:** Write all the zeros from **40** and **700** ——▶ 40 × 700 = 28,**000**

10. Multiply the one-digit numbers to find the product of the tens and hundreds.

a) 8 × 4 = ____32____

80 × 400 = ____32,000____

b) 4 × 3 = _____

40 × 300 = _____

c) 5 × 9 = _____

50 × 900 = _____

d) 2 × 6 = _____

20 × 600 = _____

e) 4 × 7 = _____

40 × 700 = _____

f) 8 × 5 = _____

80 × 500 = _____

**BONUS ▶** Estimate 3,128 × 4,956 by rounding each number first: 3,000 × 5,000 = _____

11. Multiply.

a) 30 × 200 = _____

b) 400 × 20 = _____

c) 70 × 300 = _____

# 4. Multiplying by Powers of 10

Remember: Multiplication is a short form for repeated addition: $5 \times 3 = 3 + 3 + 3 + 3 + 3$

Add five 3s

A **power** is a short form for repeated multiplication: $3^5 = 3 \times 3 \times 3 \times 3 \times 3$

Multiply five 3s

The **exponent** in a power tells you how many times to write the **base** in the product.

base $\longrightarrow 3^5 \longleftarrow$ exponent

1. Write the exponent and base for the power.

   a) $4^3$   base: ___4___          b) $5^7$   base: _____          c) $7^3$   base: _____

   exponent: ___3___                    exponent: _____                    exponent: _____

2. Write the power as a product.

   a) $8^2 =$ ___$8 \times 8$___          b) $6^3 =$ _____          c) $7^5 =$ _____

   d) $2^4 =$ _____          e) $1^5 =$ _____          f) $0^2 =$ _____

3. Write the product as a power.

   a) $4 \times 4 \times 4 =$ ___$4^3$___          b) $3 \times 3 \times 3 \times 3 =$ _____          c) $9 \times 9 =$ _____

   d) $2 \times 2 \times 2 \times 2 \times 2 =$ _____          e) $0 \times 0 \times 0 =$ _____          **BONUS** ▶ $13 \times 13 \times 13 =$ _____

**REMINDER** ▶ Multiplication is performed from left to right.

4. Evaluate the power. Write the products in the boxes as you go.

   a)
   
   | 9 | 27 | ☐ | ☐ |
   
   $3^5 = 3 \times 3 \times 3 \times 3 \times 3 =$ ☐

   b)
   
   ☐ ☐ ☐ ☐
   
   $2^4 = 2 \times 2 \times 2 \times 2 =$ ☐

   c)
   
   ☐ ☐ ☐ ☐ ☐ ☐ ☐ ☐
   
   $1^{10} = 1 \times 1 \times 1 \times 1 \times 1 \times 1 \times 1 \times 1 \times 1 \times 1 =$ ☐

   d)
   
   ☐ ☐ ☐ ☐
   
   $10^5 = 10 \times 10 \times 10 \times 10 \times 10 =$ ☐

**BONUS** ▶ Predict:   a) $1^{50} =$ _____          b) $10^9 =$ _____

5. Write the power of 10 in expanded form.

   a) $10^3 =$ _____$10 \times 10 \times 10$_____  b) $10^6 =$ _____

   c) $10^2 =$ _____  d) $10^5 =$ _____

   e) $10^8 =$ _____  f) $10^7 =$ _____

6. Write the product as a power of 10.

   a) $10 \times 10 \times 10 =$ __$10^3$__  b) $10 \times 10 \times 10 \times 10 \times 10 =$ _____

   c) $10 \times 10 =$ _____  d) $10 \times 10 \times 10 \times 10 \times 10 \times 10 \times 10 =$ _____

   e) $10 =$ _____  f) $10 \times 10 \times 10 \times 10 \times 10 \times 10 =$ _____

7. Write the number as a power of 10.

   a) $1,000 =$ __$10^3$__  b) $100,000 =$ _____

   c) $1,000,000 =$ _____  d) $100 =$ _____

   e) $10,000 =$ _____  f) $1,000,000,000 =$ _____

---

Fred multiplied the number 7 by increasing powers of 10:

| Product | Expanded Form | Product with the Power of 10 | Answer | Zeros after the Digit 7 |
|---|---|---|---|---|
| $7 \times 10$ | $7 \times 10$ | $7 \times 10^1$ | 70 | 1 |
| $7 \times 100$ | $7 \times 10 \times 10$ | $7 \times 10^2$ | 700 | 2 |
| $7 \times 1,000$ | $7 \times 10 \times 10 \times 10$ | $7 \times 10^3$ | 7,000 | 3 |
| $7 \times 10,000$ | $7 \times 10 \times 10 \times 10 \times 10$ | $7 \times 10^4$ | 70,000 | 4 |

Fred noticed that the number of zeros added after the digit 7 was the same as the exponent!

---

8. Use the exponent to find the product.

   a) $5 \times 10^3 =$ __5,000__  b) $8 \times 10^2 =$ _____  c) $7 \times 10^4 =$ _____

   d) $3 \times 10^1 =$ _____  e) $9 \times 10^5 =$ _____  f) $3 \times 10^6 =$ _____

9. Multiply.

   a) $37 \times 10^3 =$ __37,000__  b) $24 \times 10^2 =$ _____  c) $83 \times 10^4 =$ _____

   d) $50 \times 10^2 =$ _____  e) $80 \times 10^4 =$ _____  f) $90 \times 10^1 =$ _____

   BONUS ▶ $5,000 \times 10^3 =$ _____

# 5. Arrays and Multiplication

1. Write a product for the array.

a)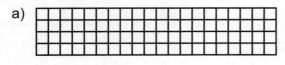

   _____4 × 20_____

b)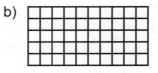

   _____

c)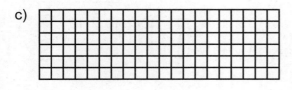

   _____

d)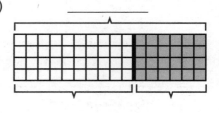

   _____

2. Write a product for the whole array and for each part of the array.

a)

   _____3 × 23_____

   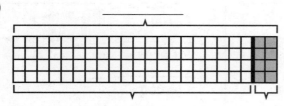

   _____3 × 20_____    _____3 × 3_____

b)

   _____

   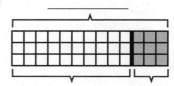

   _____    _____

c)

   _____

   _____    _____

d)

   _____

   _____    _____

3. Fill in the blanks as shown.

a)

   _____4 × 23_____

   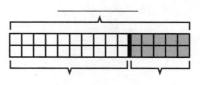

   _____4 × 20_____    _____4 × 3_____

   _____4 × 23 = (4 × 20) + (4 × 3)_____

b)

   _____

   _____    _____

   _____

c)

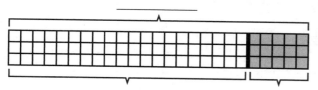

d)

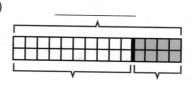

_____     _____     _____     _____     _____

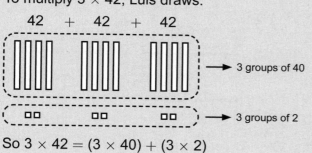

To multiply 3 × 42, Luis draws:

42   +   42   +   42

→ 3 groups of 40

→ 3 groups of 2

So 3 × 42 = (3 × 40) + (3 × 2)

Maria draws:

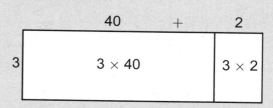

So 3 × 42 = (3 × 40) + (3 × 2)

**4.** Write a multiplication equation for the picture.

a)

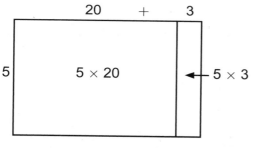

_____ $5 × 23 = (5 × 20) + (5 × 3)$ _____

b)

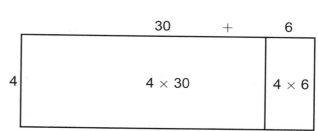

_____ $4 × 36 = ( \quad × \quad ) + ( \quad × \quad )$ _____

c)

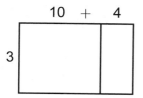

_____

d)

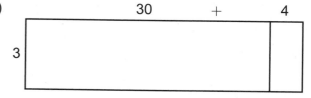

_____

**5.** Rewrite the product in expanded form.

a) $4 × 62 = (4 × \underline{\ 60\ }) + (4 × \underline{\ 2\ })$

b) $2 × 73 = (2 × \underline{\hspace{1cm}}) + (2 × \underline{\hspace{1cm}})$

c) $5 × 41 = (5 × \underline{\hspace{1cm}}) + (5 × \underline{\hspace{1cm}})$

d) $3 × 32 = (3 × \underline{\hspace{1cm}}) + (3 × \underline{\hspace{1cm}})$

e) $2 × 84 = (\underline{\hspace{1cm}} × \underline{\hspace{1cm}}) + (\underline{\hspace{1cm}} × \underline{\hspace{1cm}})$

f) $5 × 91 = (\underline{\hspace{1cm}} × \underline{\hspace{1cm}}) + (\underline{\hspace{1cm}} × \underline{\hspace{1cm}})$

g) $3 × 52 = $ _____

h) $7 × 64 = $ _____

To multiply 42 × 3 (or 3 × 42), Luis uses 3 steps.

| | | 2 |
|---|---|---|
| × | | 3 |
| | | 6 |

| | 4 | 0 |
|---|---|---|
| × | | 3 |
| 1 | 2 | 0 |

**Step 1:** Multiply 2 by 3.     2 × 3 =     6

**Step 2:** Multiply 40 by 3.     40 × 3 =     + 120

**Step 3:** Add the results.     126

| | | 2 |
|---|---|---|
| × | | 3 |
| | | 6 |
| + 1 | 2 | 0 |
| 1 | 2 | 6 |

**6.** Use Luis's steps to multiply.

a) 62 × **4**
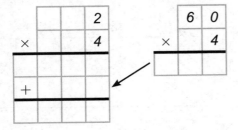

b) 73 × **2**
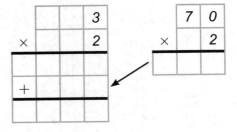

c) 41 × **5**
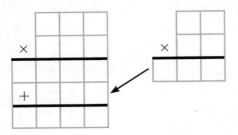

d) 32 × **3**
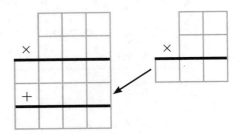

e) 32 × **6**
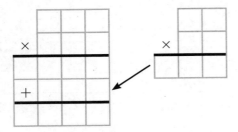

f) 54 × **7**
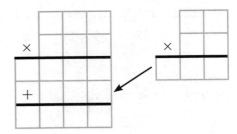

g) 71 × **8**
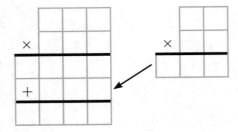

h) 62 × **9**

# 6. Standard Method for Multiplication

Chu uses a grid to multiply 42 × 3:

**Step 1**
She multiplies
the ones digit of 42 by 3.
(3 × 2 = 6)

**Step 2**
She multiplies
the tens digit of 42 by 3.
(3 × 4 tens = 12 tens)

**1.** Use Chu's method to find the product.

a) 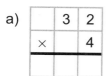  b) 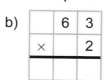  c) 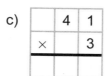  d) 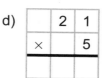  e)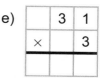

f) 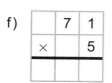  g) 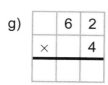  h) 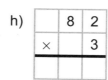  i) 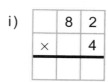  j)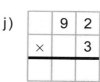

Ty multiplies $\begin{array}{r} 24 \\ \times\ 3 \\ \hline \end{array}$ in three steps: $\begin{array}{r} 20 \\ \times\ 3 \\ \hline 60 \end{array}$ + $\begin{array}{r} 4 \\ \times 3 \\ \hline \textcircled{1}2 \end{array}$ = 72  but there is a shorter way!

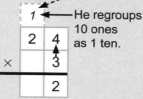

**Step 1**
He multiplies 4 ones by 3.
(4 × 3 = 12)

He regroups
10 ones
as 1 ten.

**Step 2**
He multiplies 2 tens by 3.
(3 × 2 tens = 6 tens)

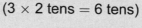

He adds 1 ten to the →
result (6 + 1 = 7 tens).

**2.** Using Ty's new method, complete the first step of the multiplication.

a) 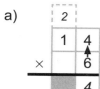  b) 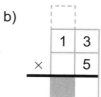  c) 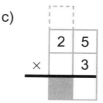  d) 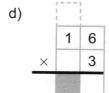  e)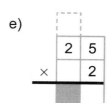

**3.** Using Ty's new method, complete the second step of the multiplication.

a) 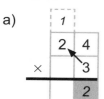  b) 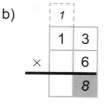  c) 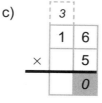  d)  e)

**4.** Using Ty's new method, complete both steps of the multiplication.

a)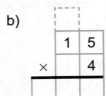

```
    1 7
×     3
───────
```

b)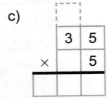

```
    1 5
×     4
───────
```

c)

```
    3 5
×     5
───────
```

d)

```
    3 5
×     4
───────
```

e)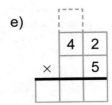

```
    4 2
×     5
───────
```

f)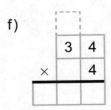

```
    3 4
×     4
───────
```

g)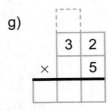

```
    3 2
×     5
───────
```

h)

```
    3 7
×     4
───────
```

i)

```
    8 7
×     3
───────
```

j)

```
    2 6
×     4
───────
```

**5.** Multiply.

a)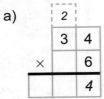

```
  2
  3 4
×   6
─────
    4
```

b)

```
  4 5
×   6
─────
```

c)

```
  5 6
×   6
─────
```

d)

```
  6 7
×   6
─────
```

e)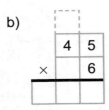

```
  7 8
×   6
─────
```

f)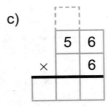

```
  7
  8 9
×   8
─────
    2
```

g)

```
  7 6
×   8
─────
```

h)

```
  5 9
×   8
─────
```

i)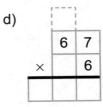

```
  9 4
×   8
─────
```

j)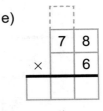

```
  7 8
×   8
─────
```

k)

```
  8
  7 9
×   9
─────
    1
```

l)

```
  6 8
×   9
─────
```

m)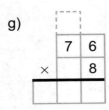

```
  2 8
×   9
─────
```

n)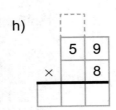

```
  7 5
×   9
─────
```

o)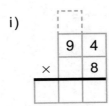

```
  4 2
×   9
─────
```

p)

```
  4
  3 6
×   7
─────
    2
```

q)

```
  4 8
×   7
─────
```

r)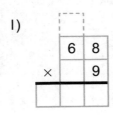

```
  2 7
×   7
─────
```

s)

```
  8 1
×   7
─────
```

t)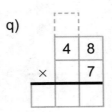

```
  1 8
×   7
─────
```

**6.** Multiply.

a) 23 × 5      b) 4 × 72      c) 6 × 81      d) 43 × 7      e) 92 × 8

f) 12 × 9      g) 3 × 75      h) 2 × 98      i) 54 × 4      j) 36 × 6

k) 5 × 25      l) 8 × 47      m) 83 × 7      n) 49 × 9      o) 98 × 8

# 7. Multiplying a Multi-Digit Number by a 1-Digit Number

Kelly multiplies $2 \times 213$ in three ways.

**With a chart:**

| hundreds | tens | ones |
|---|---|---|
| 2 | 1 | 3 |
| × |  | 2 |
| 4 | 2 | 6 |

**In expanded form:**

$$200 + 10 + 3$$
$$\underline{\times\ 2}$$
$$= 400 + 20 + 6$$
$$= 426$$

**With base ten materials:**

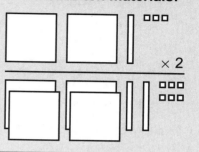

1. Rewrite the multiplication in expanded form. Then multiply.

   a) 213     _____ + _____ + _____
      × 3     _____ × 3
             = _____ + _____ + _____
             = _____

   b) 342     _____ + _____ + _____
      × 2     _____ × 2
             = _____ + _____ + _____
             = _____

2. Multiply.

   a)
   | 1 | 3 | 4 |
   |---|---|---|
   | × |  | 2 |
   |  |  |  |

   b)
   | 3 | 1 | 2 |
   |---|---|---|
   | × |  | 3 |
   |  |  |  |

   c)
   | 2 | 1 | 2 |
   |---|---|---|
   | × |  | 4 |
   |  |  |  |

   d)
   | 2 | 3 | 3 |
   |---|---|---|
   | × |  | 3 |
   |  |  |  |

   e)
   | 3 | 1 | 4 |
   |---|---|---|
   | × |  | 2 |
   |  |  |  |

3. Multiply by regrouping ones as tens.

   a)
   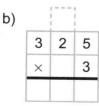
   |  | 1 |  |
   |---|---|---|
   | 1 | 2 | 3 |
   | × |  | 4 |
   | 4 | 9 | 2 |

   b)
   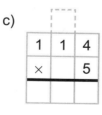
   | 3 | 2 | 5 |
   |---|---|---|
   | × |  | 3 |
   |  |  |  |

   c)
   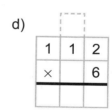
   | 1 | 1 | 4 |
   |---|---|---|
   | × |  | 5 |
   |  |  |  |

   d)
   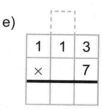
   | 1 | 1 | 2 |
   |---|---|---|
   | × |  | 6 |
   |  |  |  |

   e)
   | 1 | 1 | 3 |
   |---|---|---|
   | × |  | 7 |
   |  |  |  |

4. Multiply by regrouping tens as hundreds.

   a)
   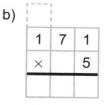
   | 1 |  |  |
   |---|---|---|
   | 2 | 4 | 1 |
   | × |  | 4 |
   | 9 | 6 | 4 |

   b)
   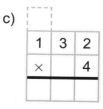
   | 1 | 7 | 1 |
   |---|---|---|
   | × |  | 5 |
   |  |  |  |

   c)
   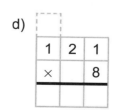
   | 1 | 3 | 2 |
   |---|---|---|
   | × |  | 4 |
   |  |  |  |

   d)
   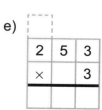
   | 1 | 2 | 1 |
   |---|---|---|
   | × |  | 8 |
   |  |  |  |

   e)
   | 2 | 5 | 3 |
   |---|---|---|
   | × |  | 3 |
   |  |  |  |

5. Use grid paper to multiply. Regroup as necessary.

   a) $437 \times 2$    b) $253 \times 4$    c) $114 \times 6$    d) $232 \times 4$    e) $141 \times 8$

Sometimes, you need to regroup hundreds as thousands. When there are no other thousands, you don't need to show the regrouping on top—you can put the regrouping in the answer right away.

Example:

|   | 2 |   |   |
|---|---|---|---|
|   | 5 | 1 | 2 |
| × |   |   | 4 |
| 2 | 0 | 4 | 8 |

You don't need to write this 2 here, because there are no other thousands to add to it.

**6.** Multiply by regrouping where necessary.

a) 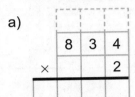  b) 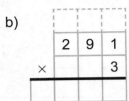  c) 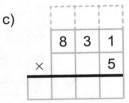  d) 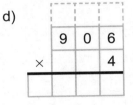  e)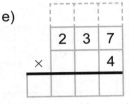

**7.** Multiply. You may need to regroup more than once.

a) 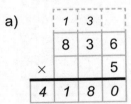  b) 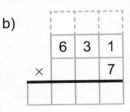  c) 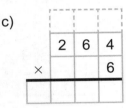  d) 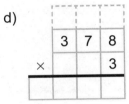  e)

**8.** Multiply by regrouping where necessary.

a)   b) 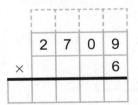  c) 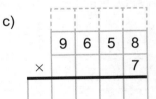  d)

e) 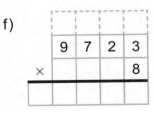  f)  **BONUS ▶**

**9.** For some species of salmon, a female lays 1,150 eggs in a nest. If a female has 5 nests, how many eggs does she lay?

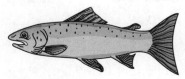

**10.** Sam types 5,700 words in one hour. How many words can he type in 8 hours?

# 8. Word Problems I

**1.** There are 1,760 yards in one mile. How many yards are in eight miles?

**2.** A household in Maine spends $248 on heating fuel each month. How much does the household spend on heating in six months?

**3.** A local school is buying televisions to put in their 5th Grade classrooms. The televisions cost $439 each. How much will the school pay to buy a television for each of their six 5th Grade classes?

**4.** Tom is working during the summer to help pay for his college textbooks. He earns $450 per week. How much will he earn in eight weeks of summer?

**5.** A school is selling raffle tickets to raise money. The average student sells $9 worth of tickets. There are 523 students in the school. How much money is raised?

**6.** There are 3,049,978 households in New York City. If there are three people in each household, what is the population of New York City?

**7.** The word "level" is a palindrome because the letters can be read forward or backward for the same result. Show that the number 412,107 multiplied by 3 is a palindrome.

**8.** A farmer's field has the shape of a pentagon. Each of its five sides is 921 feet long.

   a) What is the perimeter of the field in feet?

   b) The farmer has 4,500 feet of wire fence. How many more feet of fence will the farmer need to surround the field?

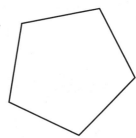

**9.** Leah spends $7 each weekday on lunch.

   a) How many weekdays are in a year?

   b) How much money does she spend for lunch in a year?

   c) Leah only budgeted $1,720 for lunch. How far over her budget was she?

**10.** A baseball stadium holds 32,459 fans. The average fan spent $8 on a ticket.

   a) How much money was spent on tickets?

   b) If the stadium could hold 33,000 fans, how much money could be spent on tickets?

## 9. Multiplying 2-Digit Numbers by Multiples of 10

Aaron wants to multiply 20 × 32.
He knows how to multiply 2 × 32.
He rewrites 20 × 32 as (10 × 2) × 32.

$$20 \times 32 = (10 \times 2) \times 32$$
$$= 10 \times (2 \times 32)$$
$$= 10 \times 64$$
$$= 640$$

The picture shows why this works.
A 20 × 32 array contains the same
number of squares as ten 2 × 32 arrays.

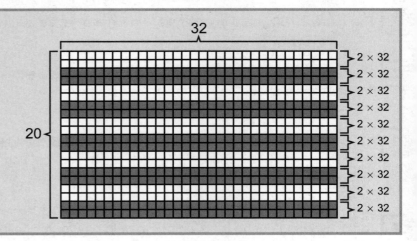

1. Find the product.

a) 30 × 21 = ( _10_ × _3_ ) × _21_

   = _10_ × ( _3_ × _21_ )

   = _10_ × _63_

   = _630_

b) 40 × 32 = (_____ × _____) × _____

   = _____ × (_____ × _____)

   = _____ × _____

   = _____

c) 70 × 21 = (_____ × _____) × _____

   = _____ × (_____ × _____)

   = _____ × _____

   = _____

d) 80 × 91 = (_____ × _____) × _____

   = _____ × (_____ × _____)

   = _____ × _____

   = _____

e) 20 × 54

f) 30 × 83

2. Find the product mentally.

a) 30 × 22 = _____   b) 20 × 41 = _____   c) 30 × 63 = _____   d) 70 × 30 = _____

e) 40 × 51 = _____   f) 60 × 31 = _____   g) 80 × 51 = _____   h) 20 × 64 = _____

3. Estimate the product. Hint: Round each number to the nearest ten.

a) 27 × 39 ≈ _____ _30 × 40 = 1,200_ _____   b) 42 × 53 ≈ _____

c) 22 × 48 ≈ _____   d) 71 × 58 ≈ _____

e) 78 × 49 ≈ _____   f) 41 × 39 ≈ _____

Annie multiplies 30 × 27 and shows her rough work:

$30 \times 27 = (10 \times 3) \times 27$

$= 10 \times (3 \times 27)$

$= 10 \times 81$

$= 810$

rough work:

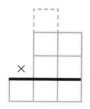

4. Show your rough work to find the product.

a) 40 × 17

$= 10 \times (\underline{\ 4\ } \times \underline{\ 17\ })$

$= 10 \times \underline{\ 68\ }$

$= \underline{\ 680\ }$

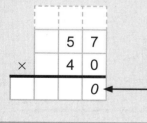

b) 30 × 24

$= 10 \times (\underline{\ \ \ } \times \underline{\ \ \ })$

$= 10 \times \underline{\ \ \ }$

$= \underline{\ \ \ }$

c) 50 × 19

$= 10 \times (\underline{\ \ \ } \times \underline{\ \ \ })$

$= 10 \times \underline{\ \ \ }$

$= \underline{\ \ \ }$

d) 20 × 36

$= 10 \times (\underline{\ \ \ } \times \underline{\ \ \ })$

$= 10 \times \underline{\ \ \ }$

$= \underline{\ \ \ }$

You can use a grid to find 40 × 57 = 10 × (4 × 57)

**Step 1:** 10 × (4 × 57)

| | | 5 | 7 |
|---|---|---|---|
| × | | 4 | 0 |
| | | | 0 |

When you multiply a number by 10, you add a zero.

So write a zero here because you will multiply 4 × 57 by ten.

**Step 2:** Multiply 4 × 57

Regroup 2 in the hundreds place because you are multiplying 7 by 40.

| | 2 | | |
|---|---|---|---|
| | | 5 | 7 |
| × | | 4 | 0 |
| 2 | 2 | 8 | 0 |

5. Multiply.

a)

| | 3 | 4 |
|---|---|---|
| × | 4 | 0 |
| | | |

b)

| | 5 | 5 |
|---|---|---|
| × | 2 | 0 |
| | | |

c)

| | 4 | 3 |
|---|---|---|
| × | 5 | 0 |
| | | |

d)

| | 2 | 5 |
|---|---|---|
| × | 7 | 0 |
| | | |

e)

| | 2 | 6 |
|---|---|---|
| × | 8 | 0 |
| | | |

6. Calculate 2,400 × 600 by breaking the product into smaller products. Explain how you found your answer.

# 10. Multiplying 2-Digit Numbers by 2-Digit Numbers

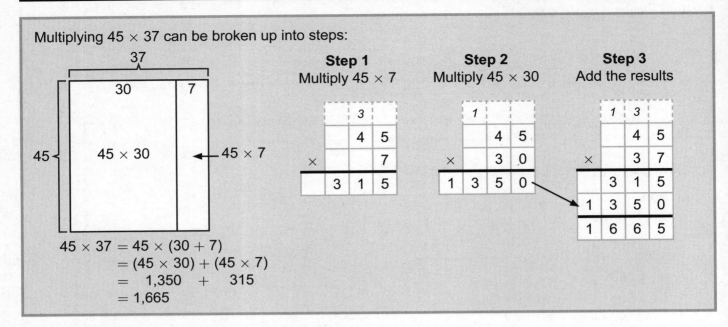

Multiplying 45 × 37 can be broken up into steps:

$$45 \times 37 = 45 \times (30 + 7)$$
$$= (45 \times 30) + (45 \times 7)$$
$$= \quad 1,350 \quad + \quad 315$$
$$= 1,665$$

**Step 1**
Multiply 45 × 7

**Step 2**
Multiply 45 × 30

**Step 3**
Add the results

**1.** Multiply, showing all three steps.

a) 64 × 35

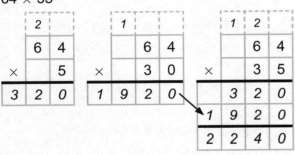

b) 26 × 45

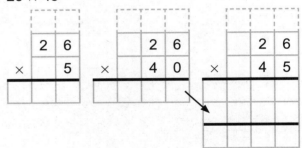

c) 53 × 42

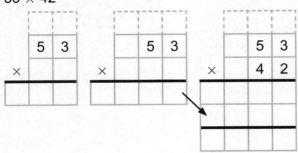

d) 78 × 32

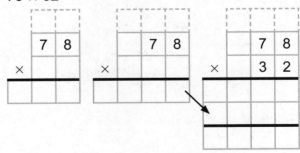

e) 87 × 38

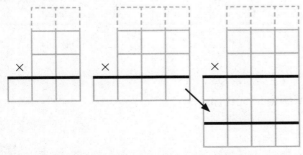

f) 98 × 26

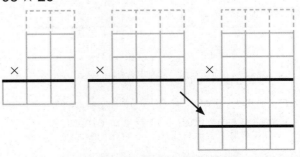

Mia multiplies 45 × 37. She uses a grid to keep track of the steps of multiplication:

**Step 1:** She multiplies 7 × 45

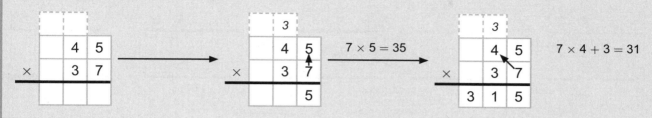

$7 \times 5 = 35$

$7 \times 4 + 3 = 31$

**2.** Practice the first step of multiplication.

a)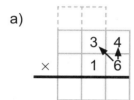

b)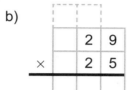

c)

d)

e)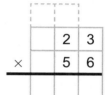

f)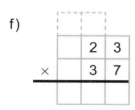

g)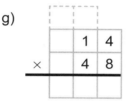

h)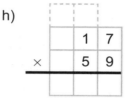

i)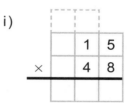

j)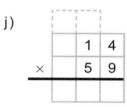

**Step 2:** Mia continues multiplying 45 × 37 by multiplying 30 × 45. Notice she starts by writing a 0 in the ones place because she is multiplying by 30, not by 3.

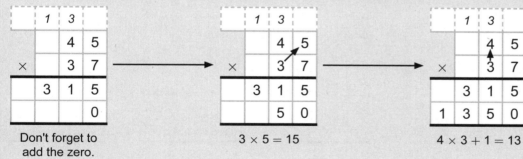

Don't forget to add the zero.

$3 \times 5 = 15$

$4 \times 3 + 1 = 13$

**3.** Practice the second step of multiplication.

a)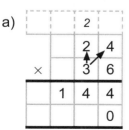

b)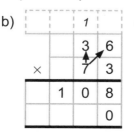

c)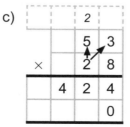

d)

e)

**4.** Practice the first and second steps of multiplication.

a)
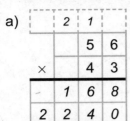

|   | *2* | *1* |   |
|---|---|---|---|
|   |   | 5 | 6 |
| × |   | 4 | 3 |
|   | 1 | 6 | 8 |
| 2 | 2 | 4 | 0 |

b)

|   |   | 3 | 4 |
|---|---|---|---|
| × |   | 2 | 7 |
|   |   |   |   |
|   |   |   |   |

c)

|   |   | 4 | 7 |
|---|---|---|---|
| × |   | 3 | 5 |
|   |   |   |   |
|   |   |   |   |

d)
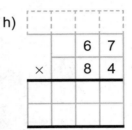

|   |   | 2 | 6 |
|---|---|---|---|
| × |   | 4 | 9 |
|   |   |   |   |
|   |   |   |   |

e)
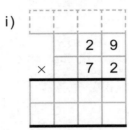

|   |   | 5 | 7 |
|---|---|---|---|
| × |   | 2 | 6 |
|   |   |   |   |
|   |   |   |   |

f)

|   |   | 2 | 3 |
|---|---|---|---|
| × |   | 7 | 4 |
|   |   |   |   |
|   |   |   |   |

g)

|   |   | 2 | 4 |
|---|---|---|---|
| × |   | 7 | 8 |
|   |   |   |   |
|   |   |   |   |

h)

|   |   | 6 | 7 |
|---|---|---|---|
| × |   | 8 | 4 |
|   |   |   |   |
|   |   |   |   |

i)

|   |   | 2 | 9 |
|---|---|---|---|
| × |   | 7 | 2 |
|   |   |   |   |
|   |   |   |   |

j)

|   |   | 2 | 4 |
|---|---|---|---|
| × |   | 8 | 3 |
|   |   |   |   |
|   |   |   |   |

**Step 3:** Mia completes the multiplication by adding the products of 45 × 7 and 45 × 30.

**5.** Practice the third step of multiplication.

a)

|   | *1* | *3* |   |
|---|---|---|---|
|   |   | 4 | 5 |
| × |   | 3 | 7 |
|   | 3 | 1 | 5 |
| 1 | 3 | 5 | 0 |
| 1 | 6 | 6 | 5 |

b)

|   | *1* | *4* |   |
|---|---|---|---|
|   |   | 3 | 8 |
| × |   | 2 | 6 |
|   | 2 | 2 | 8 |
|   | 7 | 6 | 0 |
|   |   |   |   |

c)

|   | *3* | *2* |   |
|---|---|---|---|
|   |   | 6 | 7 |
| × |   | 5 | 3 |
|   | 2 | 0 | 1 |
| 3 | 3 | 5 | 0 |
|   |   |   |   |

d)

|   | *2* | *5* |   |
|---|---|---|---|
|   |   | 7 | 6 |
| × |   | 4 | 9 |
|   | 6 | 8 | 4 |
| 3 | 0 | 4 | 0 |
|   |   |   |   |

e)

|   | *1* | *4* |   |
|---|---|---|---|
|   |   | 5 | 7 |
| × |   | 2 | 6 |
|   | 3 | 4 | 2 |
| 1 | 1 | 4 | 0 |
|   |   |   |   |

**6.** Multiply.

a)

|   |   | 2 | 9 |
|---|---|---|---|
| × |   | 5 | 4 |
|   |   |   |   |
|   |   |   |   |
|   |   |   |   |

b)

|   |   | 4 | 5 |
|---|---|---|---|
| × |   | 2 | 3 |
|   |   |   |   |
|   |   |   |   |
|   |   |   |   |

c)

|   |   | 5 | 3 |
|---|---|---|---|
| × |   | 4 | 2 |
|   |   |   |   |
|   |   |   |   |
|   |   |   |   |

d)

|   |   | 7 | 3 |
|---|---|---|---|
| × |   | 4 | 7 |
|   |   |   |   |
|   |   |   |   |
|   |   |   |   |

e)

|   |   | 5 | 4 |
|---|---|---|---|
| × |   | 3 | 9 |
|   |   |   |   |
|   |   |   |   |
|   |   |   |   |

**7.** Find the product.

a) 32 × 27    b) 65 × 37    c) 85 × 63    d) 19 × 84    e) 75 × 96    f) 89 × 46

**8.** A tree grows 54 inches in a year. How many inches does it grow in 15 years?

# 11.  Multiplying 3-Digit Numbers by 2-Digit Numbers

Multiplying 354 × 48 can be broken up into steps:

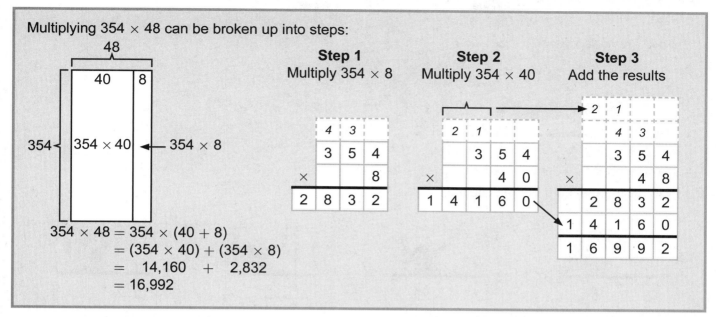

$$354 \times 48 = 354 \times (40 + 8)$$
$$= (354 \times 40) + (354 \times 8)$$
$$= \quad 14{,}160 \quad + \quad 2{,}832$$
$$= 16{,}992$$

**1.** Multiply, showing the three steps.

a)  756 × 52

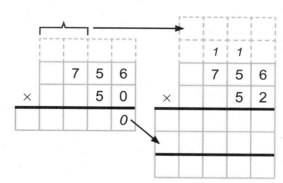

b)  328 × 46

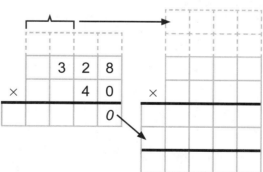

c)  572 × 29

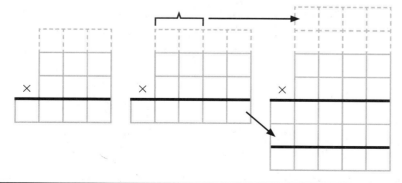

Mateo multiplies 463 × 58. He uses a grid to keep track of the steps of multiplication:

**Step 1:** He multiplies 463 × 8.

$(8 \times 4) + 5 = 37$

$8 \times 3 = 24$

$(8 \times 6) + 2 = 50$

| | 5 | 2 | |
|---|---|---|---|
| 4 | 6 | 3 |
| × | 5 | 8 |
| 3 | 7 | 0 | 4 |

**2.** Practice the first step of multiplication.

a)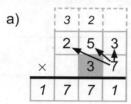

| | 3 | 2 | |
|---|---|---|---|
| 2 | 5 | 3 |
| × | 3 | 7 |
| 1 | 7 | 7 | 1 |

b)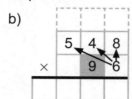

5 4 8
× 9 6

c)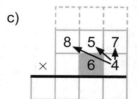

8 5 7
× 6 4

d)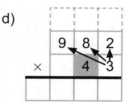

9 8 2
× 4 3

**Step 2:** Mateo continues multiplying 463 × 58 by multiplying 463 × 50. To avoid confusion with the regrouping, he crosses out the regrouping done in the first step.

$3 \times 5 = 15$

$5 \times 6 + 1 = 31$

$5 \times 4 + 3 = 23$

— Cross out the regrouping done in Step 1.

| | 3 | 1 | |
|---|---|---|---|
| | 5̸ | 2̸ | |
| 4 | 6 | 3 |
| × | 5 | 8 |
| | 3 | 7 | 0 | 4 |
| 2 | 3 | 1 | 5 | 0 |

— Don't forget the zero!

**3.** Practice the second step of multiplication.

a)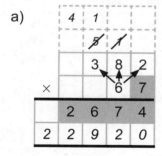

| | 4 | 1 | |
|---|---|---|---|
| | 5̸ | 1̸ | |
| 3 | 8 | 2 |
| × | 6 | 7 |
| 2 | 6 | 7 | 4 |
| 2 | 2 | 9 | 2 | 0 |

b)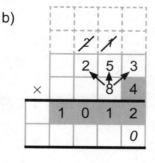

| | 2̸ | 1̸ | |
| 2 | 5 | 3 |
| × | 8 | 4 |
| 1 | 0 | 1 | 2 |
| | | | | 0 |

c)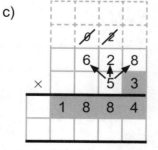

| | 0̸ | 2̸ | |
| 6 | 2 | 8 |
| × | 5 | 3 |
| 1 | 8 | 8 | 4 |

d)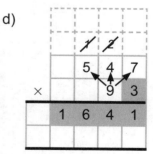

| | 1̸ | 2̸ | |
| 5 | 4 | 7 |
| × | 9 | 3 |
| 1 | 6 | 4 | 1 |

e)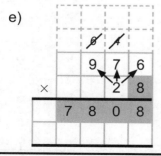

| | 6̸ | 1̸ | |
| 9 | 7 | 6 |
| × | 2 | 8 |
| 7 | 8 | 0 | 8 |

f)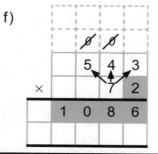

| | 0̸ | 0̸ | |
| 5 | 4 | 3 |
| × | 7 | 2 |
| 1 | 0 | 8 | 6 |

g)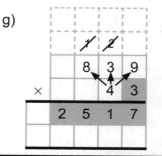

| | 1̸ | 2̸ | |
| 8 | 3 | 9 |
| × | 4 | 3 |
| 2 | 5 | 1 | 7 |

h)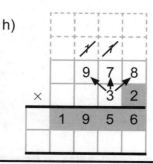

| | 1̸ | 1̸ | |
| 9 | 7 | 8 |
| × | 3 | 2 |
| 1 | 9 | 5 | 6 |

**4.** Practice steps one and two of multiplication.

a)

```
      1  1
         ✗  ✗
      8  5  7
×        2  3
   2  5  7  1
1  7  1  4  0
```

b)

```
      6  8  9
×        4  2
               0
```

c)

```
      3  2  9
×        5  7
```

d)

```
      3  2  7
×        8  6
```

e)

```
      9  2  8
×        5  4
```

f)

```
      5  2  3
×        9  1
```

g)

```
      8  0  4
×        5  6
```

h)

```
      9  1  6
×        7  5
```

---

**Step 3:** Mateo completes the multiplication by adding the products of 463 × 50 and 463 × 8.

---

**5.** Multiply.

a)

```
      4  5
         ✗  ✗
      4  5  7
×        8  3
   1  3  7  1
3  6  5  6  0
3  7  9  3  1
```

b)

```
      5  1  4
×        7  8
```

c)

```
      3  0  7
×        9  5
```

d)

```
      2  5  0
×        4  6
```

**BONUS ▶**

e)

```
      3  2  4  5
×           7  3
```

f)

```
      4  1  2  3  6  9  2
×                    4  6
```

# 12. Sequences and Multiplication (Advanced)

1. Extend the sequence by using the same operation.

   a) Subtract 3:   20, __17__, __14__, __11__   b) Multiply by 2:   5, _____, _____, _____

   c) Subtract 6:   120, _____, _____, _____   d) Multiply by 3:   2, _____, _____, _____

   e) Add 5:   2, _____, _____, _____   f) Add 12:   0, _____, _____, _____

2. Extend the sequence in both columns of the T-table.

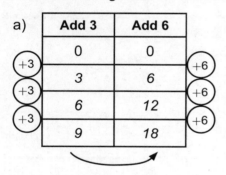

a)

| Multiply by 3 | Subtract 2 |
|---|---|
| 1 | 31 |
| 3 | 29 |
| 9 | |
| | |

b)

| Add 2 | Multiply by 2 |
|---|---|
| 3 | 3 |
| | |
| | |
| | |

c)

| Multiply by 10 | Add 100 |
|---|---|
| 1 | 81 |
| | |
| | |
| | |

3. Extend both sequences. Then write the rule for multiplying the numbers in the first column to get the numbers in the second column.

a)

| Add 3 | Add 6 |
|---|---|
| 0 | 0 |
| 3 | 6 |
| 6 | 12 |
| 9 | 18 |

Multiply by __2__

b)

| Add 2 | Add 6 |
|---|---|
| 0 | 0 |
| | |
| | |
| | |

Multiply by _____

c)

| Add 4 | Add 12 |
|---|---|
| 0 | 0 |
| | |
| | |
| | |

Multiply by _____

4. What is the rule for how you get the second sequence from the first sequence?
   Predict, and then extend the sequence to check the rule.

a)

| Add 1 | Add 6 |
|---|---|
| 0 | 0 |

Multiply by _____

b)

| Add 2 | Add 12 |
|---|---|
| 0 | 0 |

Multiply by _____

c)

| Add 10 | Add 200 |
|---|---|
| 0 | 0 |

Multiply by _____

5. Explain why the rule "Multiply by 2" works for this pair of sequences, even though they do not start with 0.

| Add 5 | Add 10 |
|---|---|
| 5 | 10 |

**6.** Extend the sequences. Then write the rule for how you get the numbers in the second column from the first column.

a)

| Multiply by 3 | Multiply by 3 |
|---|---|
| 1 | 2 |
| | |
| | |
| | |

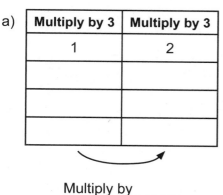

Multiply by _____

b)

| Multiply by 2 | Multiply by 2 |
|---|---|
| 2 | 6 |
| | |
| | |
| | |

Multiply by _____

c)

| Multiply by 10 | Multiply by 10 |
|---|---|
| 1 | 5 |
| | |
| | |
| | |

Multiply by _____

**7.** a) What is the rule for how you get the numbers in the second column from the first column? Predict, and then extend the sequences to check.

i)

| Multiply by 5 | Multiply by 5 |
|---|---|
| 1 | 2 |

Multiply by _____

ii)

| Multiply by 2 | Multiply by 2 |
|---|---|
| 3 | 12 |

Multiply by _____

iii)

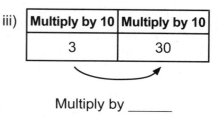

| Multiply by 10 | Multiply by 10 |
|---|---|
| 3 | 30 |

Multiply by _____

b) Explain your prediction.

**8.** Kim extended both sequences. Then she hid the numbers between the first and the last rows. What is the missing number in the last row? Hint: What is the rule for getting the numbers in the second sequence from the first?

a)

| Multiply by 10 | Multiply by 10 |
|---|---|
| 4 | 8 |
| 4,000,000 | |

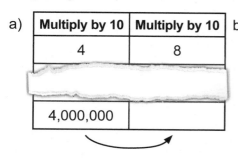

_____

b)

| Multiply by 5 | Multiply by 5 |
|---|---|
| 1 | 10 |
| 78,125 | |

_____

c)

| Multiply by 3 | Multiply by 3 |
|---|---|
| 2 | 40 |
| 1,458 | |

_____

**BONUS ▶**

a) Find the rule to go from the first sequence to the second.

b) Find the rule to go from the second sequence to the third.

c) Use these rules to make a rule to go from the first sequence to the third. Extend the sequences and check your rule.

| Add 2 | Add 10 | Add 10 |
|---|---|---|
| 0 | 0 | 1 |
| | | |

# 13. Sets

Bo has 12 veggie burgers. A tray holds 3 veggie burgers:

There are 4 trays:

The veggie burgers have been divided into 4 **sets** or **groups**.

There are 3 veggie burgers in each set.

1. a)

What has been shared or divided into sets?

_____

How many sets are there? _____

How many items are in each set? _____

b)

What has been shared or divided into sets?

_____

How many sets are there? _____

How many items are in each set? _____

2. Using circles for sets and dots for things, draw a picture to show …

a)  4 sets
    5 items in each set

b)  3 groups
    4 things in each group

c)  7 groups
    3 things in each group

d)  3 sets
    4 items in each set

**3.** Answer the questions to complete the table.

| | | What has been shared or divided into sets? | How many sets? | How many in each set? |
|---|---|---|---|---|
| a) | 24 toys<br>3 toys for each person<br>8 people | 24 toys | 8 | 3 |
| b) | 6 children<br>30 peanuts<br>5 peanuts for each child | | | |
| c) | 24 roses<br>3 bunches of flowers<br>8 roses in each bunch | | | |
| d) | 8 tomato bushes<br>56 tomatoes<br>7 tomatoes<br>   on each bush | | | |
| e) | 6 juice drinks in each pack<br>60 juice drinks<br>10 packs | | | |
| f) | 9 vans<br>72 people<br>8 people in each van | | | |
| g) | 35 eggs<br>5 eggs in a nest<br>7 nests | | | |
| h) | 6 litters of puppies<br>42 puppies<br>7 puppies in each litter | | | |

# 14. Two Ways of Sharing

Ben has 24 cookies. There are two ways he can share or **divide** his cookies equally.

**Method 1:** He can decide how many **sets** (or **groups**) of cookies he wants to make.

Example: Ben wants to make 4 sets of cookies. He draws 4 circles. He then puts one cookie at a time into the circles until he has placed all 24 cookies.

**Method 2:** He can decide how many cookies he wants to *put in each set.*

Example: Ben wants to put 8 cookies in each set. He counts out 8 cookies. He counts out sets of 8 cookies each until he has placed 24 cookies in sets.

1. Share 15 dots equally. How many dots are in each set? Hint: place one dot at a time.

   a) 3 sets:

   There are _____ dots in each set.

   b) 5 sets:

   There are _____ dots in each set.

2. Share the triangles equally among the sets. Hint: Count the triangles. Divide by the number of circles.

   a)

   b)

3. Share the squares equally among the sets.

4. Group the lines so that there are three lines in each set. How many sets are there?

   a) | | | | | |

   There are _____ sets.

   b) | | | | | | | | | | | | | |

   There are _____ sets.

   c) | | | | | | | | | | |

   There are _____ sets.

5. Group 16 leaves so that there are …

   a) 4 leaves in each set.

   b) 8 leaves in each set.

**6.** Answer the questions to complete the table. Use a question mark to show what you don't know.

| | | What has been shared or divided into sets? | How many sets? | How many in each set? |
|---|---|---|---|---|
| a) | Kathy has 48 stamps. She puts 6 stamps on each page. | 48 stamps | ? | 6 |
| b) | 24 kittens are in 4 baskets. | 24 kittens | 4 | ? |
| c) | Andy has 36 apples. He gives them to 4 friends. | | | |
| d) | Marek has 40 magazines. He puts 8 magazines on each desk. | | | |
| e) | 28 children sit at 7 tables. | | | |
| f) | 15 people are in 3 boats. | | | |
| g) | 27 baseballs are shared among 9 players. | | | |
| h) | 12 plants are in 3 rows. | | | |
| i) | 18 birds are in 6 trees. | | | |

**7.** Draw a picture using dots and circles to fill in the blank.

a) 15 dots; 5 sets

_____ dots in each set

b) 28 dots; 7 dots in each set

_____ sets

c) 35 dots; 7 dots in each set

_____ sets

d) 18 dots; 3 sets

_____ dots in each set

e) 4 friends share 12 strawberries.

How many strawberries does each get? _____

f) 30 students paddle 10 canoes.

How many are in each canoe? _____

g) Nina has 21 pencils.
She gives 7 pencils to each friend.

How many friends get pencils? _____

h) Each basket holds 8 peaches.
There are 32 peaches altogether.

How many baskets are there? _____

i) 18 flowers are planted in 2 pots.

How many flowers are in each pot? _____

j) Ken has 21 pictures for his scrapbook.
He puts 3 pictures on each page.

How many pages does he use? _____

# 15. Division, Addition, and Multiplication

Every division equation can be rewritten as an *addition equation*.

Example: "15 divided into sets of size 3 equals 5 sets" is written as $15 \div 3 = 5$.

The addition can be shown in two ways:

as a picture with dots          and          by skip counting on a number line.

          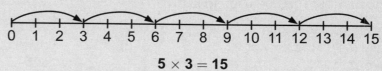

$3 + 3 + 3 + 3 + 3 = 15$          $5 \times 3 = 15$

1. Draw a picture using dots and write an addition equation for the division equation.

   a) $12 \div 3 = 4$

   b) $10 \div 5 = 2$

   _____          _____

2. Skip count on the number line and write an addition equation for the division equation.

   a) $10 \div 2 = 5$

   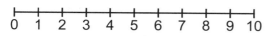

   b) $12 \div 6 = 2$

   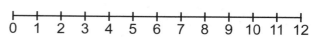

   _____          _____

3. Write an addition equation for the division equation.

   a) $20 \div 4 = 5$          b) $21 \div 7 = 3$          c) $32 \div 8 = 4$          d) $45 \div 9 = 5$

   _____          _____          _____          _____

4. Write a division equation for the addition equation.

   a) $6 + 6 + 6 = 18$          b) $8 + 8 + 8 + 8 + 8 = 40$          c) $1 + 1 + 1 + 1 + 1 + 1 = 6$

   _____          _____          _____

**BONUS ▶**

   d) $1 + 1 + 1 + 1 + 1 + 1 + 1 + 1 + 1 + 1 + 1 + 1 + 1 + 1 + 1 = 15$          _____

   e) $200,000 + 200,000 + 200,000 + 200,000 + 200,000 = 1,000,000$          _____

We can look at the diagram  in rows or columns

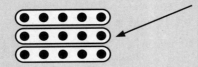

This diagram can be used to show:

- We are adding three 5s to get 15. This gives us the equations $5 + 5 + 5 = 15$ or **3 5 15**

- We are dividing 15 into sets of size 5 to get 3 sets. This gives the equation **15 5 3**.

This diagram can be used to show:

- We are adding five 3s to get 15. This gives us the equations $3 + 3 + 3 + 3 + 3 = 15$ or **5 3 15**

- We are dividing 15 into sets of size 3 to get 5 sets. This gives the equation **15 3 5**.

So the diagram  gives us a **fact family of equations**:

| | |
|---|---|
| $3 \times 5 = 15$ | $5 \times 3 = 15$ |
| $15 \div 5 = 3$ | $15 \div 3 = 5$ |

5. Write two multiplication equations for the division equation.

a) $15 \div 3 = 5$

$\underline{5 \times 3 = 15}$

$\underline{3 \times 5 = 15}$

b) $24 \div 4 = 6$

_____

_____

c) $36 \div 9 = 4$

_____

_____

d) $56 \div 7 = 8$

_____

_____

6. Write two division equations for the multiplication equation.

a) $7 \times 3 = 21$

$\underline{21 \div 3 = 7}$

$\underline{21 \div 7 = 3}$

b) $8 \times 4 = 32$

_____

_____

c) $5 \times 9 = 45$

_____

_____

d) $5 \times 7 = 35$

_____

_____

7. Find the missing number in the multiplication equation. Use it to find the answer to the division equation.

a) $4 \times \boxed{5} = 20$

$20 \div 4 = \boxed{5}$

b) $6 \times \boxed{\phantom{0}} = 18$

$18 \div 6 = \boxed{\phantom{0}}$

c) $7 \times \boxed{\phantom{0}} = 35$

$35 \div 7 = \boxed{\phantom{0}}$

d) $6 \times \boxed{\phantom{0}} = 54$

$54 \div 6 = \boxed{\phantom{0}}$

e) $8 \times \boxed{\phantom{0}} = 48$

$48 \div 8 = \boxed{\phantom{0}}$

f) $7 \times \boxed{\phantom{0}} = 42$

$42 \div 7 = \boxed{\phantom{0}}$

g) $3 \times \boxed{\phantom{0}} = 24$

$24 \div 3 = \boxed{\phantom{0}}$

h) $5 \times \boxed{\phantom{0}} = 45$

$45 \div 5 = \boxed{\phantom{0}}$

# 16. Remainders

Marisa wants to share 14 almonds with 3 friends.
She sets out four plates, one for herself and one for each of her friends.
She puts one almond at a time on each plate:

There are two almonds left over.

14 almonds cannot be divided equally into four sets. Each friend gets three almonds but two almonds are left over.

$$14 \div 4 = 3 \text{ Remainder } 2$$

1. Can 3 people share 7 strawberries equally? Show your work using dots and circles.

2. Share the dots as equally as possible among the circles.

   a) 7 dots in 2 circles

   _3_ dots in each circle; _1_ dot remaining

   b) 13 dots in 3 circles

   ____ dots in each circle; ____ dot remaining

   c) 14 dots in 5 circles

   ____ dots in each circle; ____ dots remaining

   d) 9 dots in 2 circles

   ____ dots in each circle; ____ dot remaining

   e) 20 dots in 3 circles

   ____ dots in each circle; ____ dots remaining

   f) 13 dots in 4 circles

   ____ dots in each circle; ____ dot remaining

3. Share the dots as equally as possible. Draw a picture and write a division equation.

a) 7 dots in 3 circles

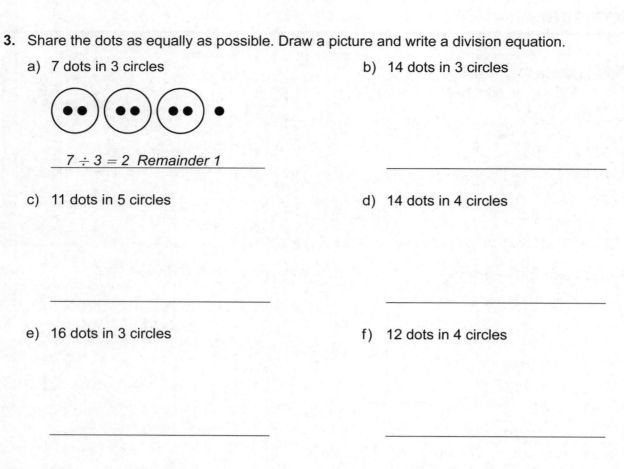

$7 \div 3 = 2$  *Remainder 1*

b) 14 dots in 3 circles

_____

c) 11 dots in 5 circles

_____

d) 14 dots in 4 circles

_____

e) 16 dots in 3 circles

_____

f) 12 dots in 4 circles

_____

4. Four friends want to share 11 cherries. How many cherries will each friend receive? How many will be left over or remaining? Show your work and write a division equation.

5. Find two different ways to share 21 granola bars into equal groups so that one is left over.

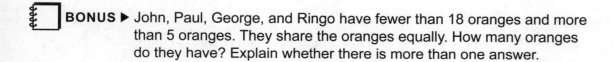

**BONUS ▶** John, Paul, George, and Ringo have fewer than 18 oranges and more than 5 oranges. They share the oranges equally. How many oranges do they have? Explain whether there is more than one answer.

## 17. Finding Remainders on Number Lines

Quinn has 14 oranges. He wants to sell them in bags of 3. He skip counts to find out how many bags he can sell.

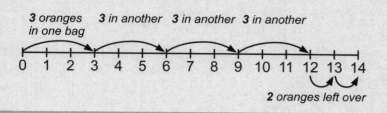

**14** oranges divided into sets of size **3** gives **4** sets and **2** oranges **remaining**.

$14 \div 3 = 4$ **Remainder 2**

*size of skip*   *number of skip*

**1.** Fill in the missing numbers.

a)
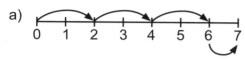

Size of skip = _____

Number of skips = _____

Remainder = _____

b)
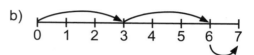

Size of skip = _____

Number of skips = _____

Remainder = _____

c)
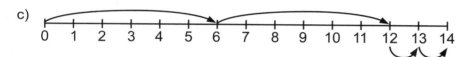

Size of skip = _____          Number of skips = _____          Remainder = _____

**2.** Write the division equation.

a)
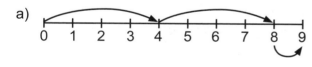

_____

b)
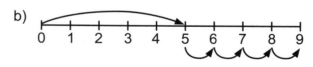

_____

**3.** Sofia has 10 pears. She wants to make bags of 4.

How many bags can she make? _____

How many pears will be left over? _____

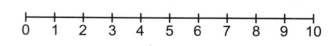

The equation $7 \div 3 = 2$ Remainder 1 can also be written as $7 \div 3 = 2$ R 1.

**4.** On grid paper, draw a number line to show the division equation.

a) $7 \div 2 = 3$ R 1

b) $11 \div 4 = 2$ R 3

c) $14 \div 5 = 2$ R 4

Camille wants to find 13 ÷ 5 mentally.

**Step 1:** Camille counts by fives. She stops when counting more would pass 13.

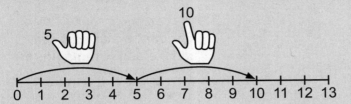

*She has two fingers up.*

$13 ÷ 5 =$ ___2___ R ____

**Step 2:** Camille stops counting at 10. She subtracts 10 from 13 to find the remainder.

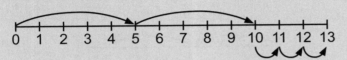

$13 ÷ 5 =$ ___2___ R ___3___

5. Divide by skip counting.

a) $18 ÷ 5 =$ _____ R _____

b) $22 ÷ 5 =$ _____ R _____

c) $27 ÷ 5 =$ _____ R _____

d) $23 ÷ 5 =$ _____ R _____

e) $14 ÷ 5 =$ _____ R _____

f) $6 ÷ 5 =$ _____ R _____

g) $11 ÷ 3 =$ _____ R _____

h) $3 ÷ 3 =$ _____ R _____

i) $17 ÷ 3 =$ _____ R _____

j) $10 ÷ 2 =$ _____ R _____

k) $7 ÷ 2 =$ _____ R _____

l) $19 ÷ 4 =$ _____ R _____

m) $23 ÷ 7 =$ _____ R _____

n) $19 ÷ 9 =$ _____ R _____

o) $23 ÷ 9 =$ _____ R _____

p) $17 ÷ 8 =$ _____ R _____

q) $26 ÷ 8 =$ _____ R _____

r) $39 ÷ 7 =$ _____ R _____

6. Ricardo wants to divide 13 pencils among 5 friends.

   How many pencils will each friend get? _____

   How many will be left over? _____

7. You have 19 tickets for rides at an amusement park. Each ride takes 5 tickets.

   How many rides can you go on? _____

   How many tickets will be left over? _____

8. There are 23 students in a class. There are 5 desks in each row.

   How many rows of desks are needed? _____

   How many desks will be empty? _____

# 18. Long Division

Isabella is preparing snacks for 4 classes. She needs to divide 94 apples into 4 groups. She uses long division and a model to solve the problem.

**Step 1:** Write the numbers like this:

the number of groups ⟶ 4)94 ⟵ the number of objects to divide into groups

$94 = 9$ tens $+ 4$ ones

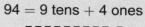

1. Fill in the blanks for the division statement.

   a) 3)74

   _____ groups

   _____ tens

   _____ ones

   b) 4)21

   _____ groups

   _____ tens

   _____ ones

   c) 4)91

   _____ groups

   _____ tens

   _____ ones

   d) 5)89

   _____ groups

   _____ tens

   _____ ones

**Step 2:** How many tens can Isabella put in each group?

2 tens in each group ⟶ **2**

4 groups ⟶ 4)9 4

2. Write how many groups have been made and how many tens are in each group.

   a) 
   ```
     2
   3)7 4
   ```
   __3__ groups

   __2__ tens in each group

   b) 
   ```
   5)9 3
   ```
   _____ groups

   _____ ten in each group

   c) 
   ```
   3)8 2
   ```
   _____ groups

   _____ tens in each group

   d) 
   ```
   4)7 5
   ```
   _____ groups

   _____ ten in each group

3. How many tens can be put in each group?

   a) 
   ```
     2
   3)7 9
   ```

   b) 
   ```
   2)7 8
   ```

   c) 
   ```
   4)9 1
   ```

   d) 
   ```
   5)6 8
   ```

   e) 
   ```
   2)9 7
   ```

   f) 
   ```
   3)6 5
   ```

   g) 
   ```
   7)8 0
   ```

   h) 
   ```
   5)9 8
   ```

**Step 3:** How many tens can Isabella place into groups altogether?

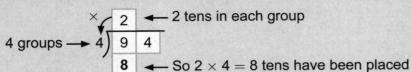

× 2 ← 2 tens in each group

4 groups → 4)9 4

8 ← So 2 × 4 = 8 tens have been placed

4. Multiply to decide how many tens have been placed.

a)
```
    3
2) 7  5
   6
```

b)
```
    2
3) 8  3
```

c)
```
    2
4) 9  7
```

d)
```
    1
5) 6  3
```

5. Multiply to decide how many tens have been placed. Then answer the questions.

a)
```
    3
2) 7  5
   6
```

b)
```
    2
3) 8  3
```

How many groups? _____

How many tens? _____

How many tens in each group? _____

How many tens placed altogether? _____

How many groups? _____

How many tens? _____

How many tens in each group? _____

How many tens placed altogether? _____

6. Skip count to find out how many tens can be placed in each group. Then multiply to find out how many tens have been placed.

a)
```
    4
2) 9  3
   8
```

b)
```
3) 7  5
```

c)
```
4) 9  7
```

d)
```
5) 6  4
```

e)
```
3) 8  5
```

f)
```
4) 7  8
```

g)
```
5) 9  4
```

h)
```
6) 7  1
```

**Step 4:** How many tens does Isabella have left over?

There are 9 tens.

Isabella has placed 8 tens. ───────────▶

9 − 8 = 1 ten is left over ───────────▶

9 tens − 8 tens = 1 ten left over

7. Carry out the first four steps of long division.

a)

```
      2
  3) 7  4
   − 6
     ───
      1
```

b)

```
  2) 9  5
   −
     ───
```

c)

```
  4) 9  7
   −
     ───
```

d)

```
  5) 8  3
   −
     ───
```

e)

```
  6) 7  3
   −
     ───
```

f)

```
  2) 7  1
   −
     ───
```

g)

```
  3) 4  6
   −
     ───
```

h)

```
  2) 5  8
   −
     ───
```

**Step 5:** 1 ten and 4 ones are left over.

So there are 14 ones left over.

Write 4 beside the 1 to show this.

There are 14 ones still to place ───▶

8. Carry out the first five steps of long division.

a)

```
      4
  2) 9  1
   − 8
     ─────
     1   1
```

b)

```
  3) 8  5
   −
     ─────
```

c)

```
  4) 7  5
   −
     ─────
```

d)

```
  5) 7  2
   −
     ─────
```

e)

```
  8) 9  3
   −
     ─────
```

f)

```
  2) 7  9
   −
     ─────
```

g)

```
  3) 7  4
   −
     ─────
```

h)

```
  4) 6  7
   −
     ─────
```

**Step 6:** How many of the 14 ones can Isabella place in each group?

Divide to find out.

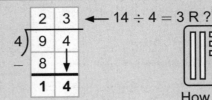 ← 14 ÷ 4 = 3 R ?

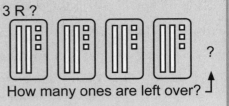

How many ones are left over? ↰

9. Carry out the first six steps of long division.

a)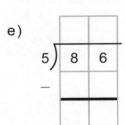

b)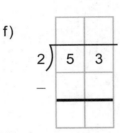

c)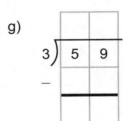

d)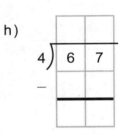

e)  5)8 6

f)  2)5 3

g)  3)5 9

h)  4)6 7

**Step 7:** How many ones are left over?

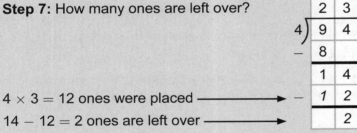 ← 3 ones in each group and 4 groups

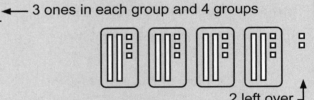

2 left over ↰

4 × 3 = 12 ones were placed ──→

14 − 12 = 2 ones are left over ──→

**94 ÷ 4 = 23 with 2 left over**

10. Carry out all seven steps of long division.

a)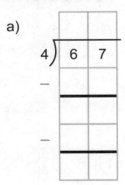

b)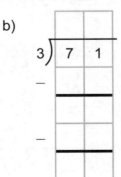

c)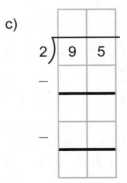

d)  5)8 3

**11.** Ali jogs for 3 km every day. How many days will it take her to run 45 km?

**12.** How many weeks are in 93 days?

# 19. Long Division—Multi-Digit by 1-Digit

When drawing pictures in math, you need to make them simple.

Example: A picture of 535 shown with hundreds blocks, tens blocks, and ones blocks:

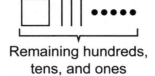

1. Use the base ten models shown to find 535 ÷ 2. Complete your answer on the right.

**Step 1:** Divide the hundreds squares into 2 equal groups.

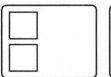 

Remaining hundreds, tens, and ones

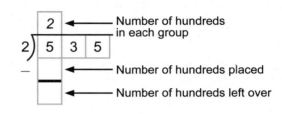

Number of hundreds in each group

Number of hundreds placed

Number of hundreds left over

**Step 2:** Exchange the leftover hundreds square for 10 tens.

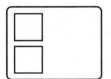 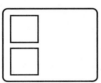

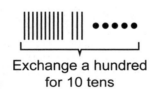

Exchange a hundred for 10 tens

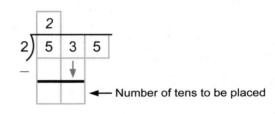

Number of tens to be placed

**Step 3:** Divide the tens blocks into 2 equal groups.
Then exchange the left over tens block for 10 ones.

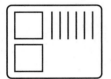 

Remaining tens and ones

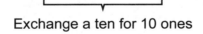

Exchange a ten for 10 ones

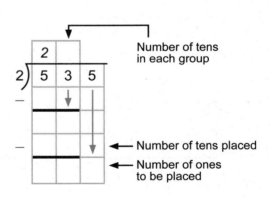

Number of tens in each group

Number of tens placed

Number of ones to be placed

**Step 4:** Divide the ones into 2 equal groups.

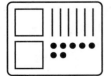 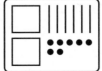

Remaining ones

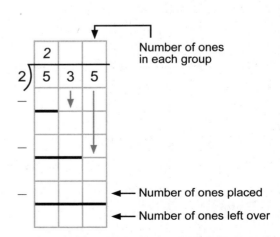

Number of ones in each group

Number of ones placed

Number of ones left over

So 535 ÷ 2 = _____ Remainder _____

**2.** Divide (without base ten models). Use the steps in Question 1.

a)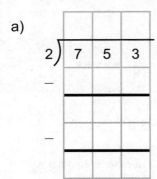

b)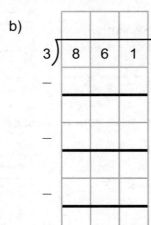

c)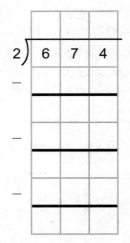

d)

**3.** Divide. There will be fewer hundreds than the number of groups. Write "0" in the hundreds position to show this. The first one has been started for you.

a)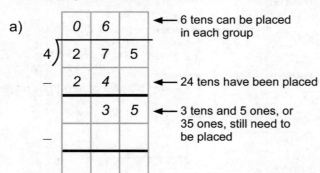

6 tens can be placed in each group

24 tens have been placed

3 tens and 5 ones, or 35 ones, still need to be placed

b)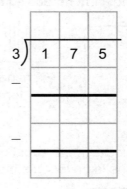

c)

d)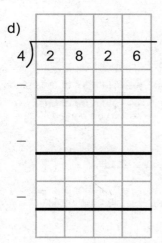

e)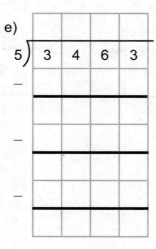

f)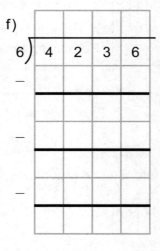

g)

**4.** Divide using long division.

a) $8{,}241 \div 3$　　b) $6{,}432 \div 5$　　c) $9{,}456 \div 4$　　d) $24{,}075 \div 3$

**5.** A boat can hold 4 children. How many boats will 372 children need?

# 20. Interpreting Remainders

For the long division

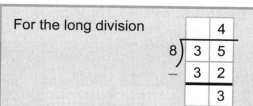

the division equation is: 35 ÷ 8 = 4   R 3

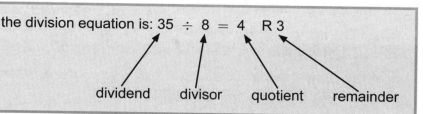

dividend   divisor   quotient   remainder

1.  Circle the quotient. Underline the remainder.

   a) 45 ÷ 7 = 6 R 3      b) 25 ÷ 3 = 8 R 1      c) 32 ÷ 9 = 3 R 5      d) 13 ÷ 2 = 6 R 1

---

Sometimes the answer to a division problem is the quotient *without* the remainder.

Example: Joanna has $14. How many $4 cartons of milk can she buy?

Solution: Skip count until one more carton would cost too much money.

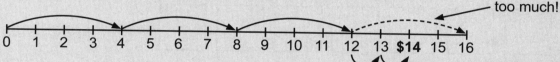

Then write the division: 14 ÷ 4 = 3 R 2. Joanna can't buy *part* of a fourth carton of milk, so ignore the remainder. The answer is the quotient: Joanna can buy 3 cartons of milk.

---

2.  Jordan has $19. How many $5 movie tickets can he buy?

   a) Skip count by $5 until the movie tickets cost too much money.

   b) How many tickets can he buy? _____

   c) How much money is left over? _____

   d) Write the division equation: 19 ÷ 5 = _____ R _____

3.  Write a division statement. Then answer the question.

   a) Ahmed has $45. How many $8 T-shirts can he buy?

   45 ÷ 8 = _____ R _____ , so he can buy _____ T-shirts and have $ _____ remaining.

   b) Nancy has $82. How many $6 books can she buy?

   _____ ÷ _____ = _____ R _____ , so she can buy _____ books and have $ _____ remaining.

4. | Nina has 26 tickets for rides at an amusement park.
   Each ride takes 3 tickets. How many rides can she go on?

Sometimes the answer to a division problem is one *greater* than the quotient.

Example: Each can holds 3 tennis balls. A tennis instructor needs 19 tennis balls.
How many cans does the instructor need to buy?

Solution: Draw 3 tennis balls in each can, until you have 19 tennis balls.

$19 \div 3 = 6$ R 1, so 6 cans are completely filled. You need 1 more can for the last ball.
So the instructor needs to buy 7 cans altogether.

5. Fred has 23 marbles. Each box holds 4 marbles.

   a) Draw 4 marbles in each box until you have 23 marbles. Then write the division equation

   _____

   b) How many boxes are completely full? _____

   c) How many boxes does Fred need to hold his marbles? _____

6. Ava needs to move 11 boxes. On each trip she can carry 4 boxes.
   How many trips will she need to make?

   _____ ÷ _____ = _____ R _____ , so Ava needs to make _____ trips.

7. Write the division statement. Interpret the remainder to answer the question.

   a) Twenty-four people are going in cars for a family trip. Each car holds 5 people.
      How many cars are needed?

   b) Jayden has $75. Each comic book costs $9. How many comic books
      can he buy?

   c) Ivan needs to raise $57. He cuts lawns for $7. How many lawns will he cut
      to raise the money?

   d) Madison has 31 kg of salt. She sells it in 2 kg bags. How many bags can
      she sell?

   e) A baseball league has 75 people. Each team needs 9 people. How many
      teams can be formed?

   f) Christie wants to place her stamps in an album. Each page holds 9 stamps.
      How many pages will she need for 87 stamps?

# 21. Concepts in Multiplication and Division

**1.** Tom bought a digital camera for each of his four children. Each camera costs $528. How much did he spend?

**2.** A school has six 5th Grade classes each with the same number of students. There are 192 5th Grade students. How many students are in each class?

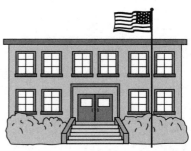

**3.** A store has enough golf balls to sell eight customers 36 golf balls each. If there were nine customers, how many golf balls could each customer buy?

**4.** Vera drives to and from work each weekday. She travels 720 km in one week. How far does she travel each day?

**5.** A ticket in a movie theater costs $9. The theater earned $3,870 in ticket sales. If the theater had charged $12 for each ticket, how much could the theater earn?

**6.** Vincente has a backyard in the shape of a square. He spent $3,840 on fencing.

a) He was charged $8 a foot for fencing. What was the perimeter of the backyard?

b) What is the width of the backyard?

**7.** Find a number which is divisible by 2, 3, 5, and 7.

**8.** A school is holding a food drive. Students are donating canned food by putting cans in boxes. Each box will hold at most six cans. How many boxes are needed for 125 cans?

**9.** Fruit juice bottles cost $3. How many bottles can be purchased with $142?

**10.** A car can hold five people. How many cars will 37 passengers need?

**11.** A sports team needs to raise $500 by washing cars. The cost of a carwash is $6. How many cars will the team need to wash?

**12.** Mia draws four pictures in her sketchbook every day. How many days will she take to draw 50 pictures?

**13.** Nine friends will equally share 76 apples they picked at a farm. How many apples will each friend get?

**14.** A bike race of 170 miles is being held on a circular course that is 4 miles long. Shahira has made 35 laps of the circuit.

a) How far has she traveled?

b) How much farther does she need to ride?

c) About how many laps does she have left?

**15.** In baseball, a pitcher pitches every fifth game. In a season of 162 games, what is the greatest number of games in which a pitcher can pitch?

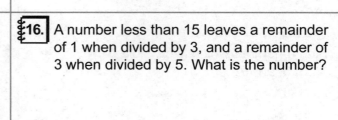

**16.** A number less than 15 leaves a remainder of 1 when divided by 3, and a remainder of 3 when divided by 5. What is the number?

# 22. Naming Fractions and Models of Fractions

The pie is cut into 4 equal parts.

3 parts out of 4 are shaded.

$\frac{3}{4}$ of the pie is shaded.

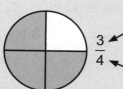

The **numerator** (3) tells you how many parts are shaded.

$\frac{3}{4}$

The **denominator** (4) tells you how many equal parts are in a whole.

1. Name the fraction.

a)

b)

c)

d)

e)

f)

g)

h)

2. Shade the given fraction.

a) $\frac{3}{6}$

b) $\frac{2}{5}$

c) $\frac{5}{9}$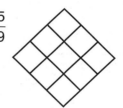

3. Use one of the following words to describe the parts in the models below.

**halves    thirds    fourths    fifths    sixths    sevenths    eighths    ninths**

a)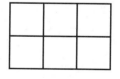

_____

b)

_____

c)

_____

d)

_____

e)

_____

f)

_____

4. Sketch a circle cut in …

a) thirds

b) quarters (or fourths)

c) eighths

**5.** Use a centimeter ruler to divide the line into the given number of equal parts.

a) 5 equal part

b) 3 equal parts

c) 4 equal parts

_____  _____  _____

d) 7 equal parts

e) 8 equal parts

_____  _____

**6.** Use a centimeter ruler to divide the box into the given number of equal parts.

a) 4 equal parts

b) 5 equal parts

c) 3 equal parts

d) 6 equal parts

**7.** Using a centimeter ruler, find what fraction of the box is shaded.

a)

is shaded

b)

is shaded

c)

is shaded

d)

is shaded

**8.** Using a centimeter ruler, complete the figure to make a whole.

a) $\dfrac{1}{2}$

b) $\dfrac{1}{3}$

c) $\dfrac{1}{4}$

**9.** You have $\dfrac{3}{5}$ of a pie.

a) What does the bottom (denominator) of the fraction tell you?

b) What does the top (numerator) of the fraction tell you?

**10.** Explain why the picture does (or does not) show $\dfrac{1}{4}$.

a)

b)

c)

d)

# 23. Equal Parts of a Set

Fractions can name or describe parts of a set: $\frac{3}{5}$ of the shapes are triangles, $\frac{1}{5}$ are squares, $\frac{1}{5}$ are circles.

1. Complete the sentences.

   a)

   of the shapes are triangles.

   of the shapes are shaded.

   b)

   of the shapes are squares.

   of the shapes are shaded.

2. Complete the sentence.

   a) $\frac{4}{7}$ of the shapes are _____.

   b) $\frac{2}{7}$ of the shapes are _____.

   c) $\frac{1}{7}$ of the shapes are _____.

   d) $\frac{3}{7}$ of the shapes are _____.

3. Describe the picture in two different ways using the fraction $\frac{3}{5}$.

   _____

   _____

4. A football team wins 7 games and loses 5 games.

   a) How many games did the team play? _____

   b) What *fraction* of the games did the team win? ☐

   c) Did the team win more than half its games? _____

5. Answer the question using the information in the table.

|  | Number of girls | Number of boys |
|---|---|---|
| The Smith Family | 2 | 3 |
| The Sinha Family | 1 | 2 |

a) What fraction of the children in each family are girls?

Smiths [ ]       Sinhas [ ]

b) What fraction of all the children are girls? [ ]

6. What fraction of the letters in the word "Maine" are …

a) vowels? [ ]          b) consonants? [ ]

7. Express 7 months as a fraction of one year. [ ]

8. △ ■ ○ ○ ▨ ☐ ☐ ◉

a) [ ] of the shapes are circles.          b) [ ] of the shapes are triangles.

c) [ ] of the shapes are striped.          d) [ ] of the shapes are white.

9. Write two more fraction statements for the figures in Question 8.

[ ] of the shapes are _____.

[ ] of the shapes are _____.

10. Draw the shaded and unshaded shapes.

a) There are 7 circles and squares.

$\frac{2}{7}$ of the shapes are squares.

$\frac{5}{7}$ of the shapes are shaded.

3 circles are shaded.

b) There are 8 triangles and squares.

$\frac{6}{8}$ of the shapes are shaded.

$\frac{2}{8}$ of the shapes are triangles.

1 triangle is shaded.

# 24. Comparing and Ordering Fractions

1. What fraction has a greater numerator, $\frac{2}{6}$ or $\frac{5}{6}$ ?

   Which fraction is greater?

   Explain your thinking. _____

   _____

2. Circle the greater fraction in the pair.

   a) $\frac{6}{16}$ or $\frac{9}{16}$     b) $\frac{5}{8}$ or $\frac{3}{8}$     c) $\frac{24}{25}$ or $\frac{22}{25}$     d) $\frac{37}{53}$ or $\frac{27}{53}$

3. Two fractions have the same *denominators* (bottoms) but different *numerators* (tops).
   How can you tell which fraction is greater?

   _____

   _____

4. Circle the greater fraction in the pair.

   a) $\frac{1}{8}$ or $\frac{1}{9}$     b) $\frac{12}{12}$ or $\frac{12}{13}$     c) $\frac{5}{225}$ or $\frac{5}{125}$     d) $\frac{61}{253}$ or $\frac{61}{514}$

5. Fraction A and Fraction B have the same *numerators* but different *denominators*.
   How can you tell which fraction is greater?

   _____

   _____

6. Write the fractions in order from least to greatest.

   a) $\frac{2}{3}, \frac{1}{3}, \frac{3}{3}$  ☐ < ☐ < ☐     b) $\frac{9}{10}, \frac{2}{10}, \frac{1}{10}, \frac{5}{10}$  ☐ < ☐ < ☐ < ☐

   c) $\frac{1}{7}, \frac{1}{3}, \frac{1}{13}$  ☐ < ☐ < ☐     d) $\frac{2}{11}, \frac{2}{5}, \frac{2}{7}, \frac{2}{16}$  ☐ < ☐ < ☐ < ☐

7. Circle the greater fraction in the pair.

   a) $\frac{2}{3}$ or $\frac{2}{9}$     b) $\frac{7}{17}$ or $\frac{11}{17}$     c) $\frac{6}{288}$ or $\frac{6}{18}$     d) $\frac{93}{174}$ or $\frac{74}{174}$

8. Which fraction is greater, $\frac{1}{2}$ or $\frac{45}{100}$ ? Explain your thinking.

9. Is it possible for $\frac{2}{3}$ of a pie to be bigger than $\frac{3}{4}$ of another pie? Show your thinking
   with a picture.

# 25. Mixed Numbers and Improper Fractions (Introduction)

Mateo and his friends ate the amount of pie shown.

They ate three and one quarter pies altogether (or $3\frac{1}{4}$ pies).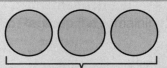

3 whole pies     and $\frac{1}{4}$ of another pie

$3\frac{1}{4}$ is called a **mixed number** because it is a *mixture* of a whole number and a fraction.

1. Write how many *whole* pies are shaded.

a)

_____2_____ whole pies

b)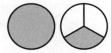

_____ whole pies

c)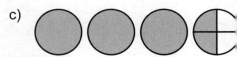

_____ whole pie

2. The shaded areas are fractions. Write the fractions as *mixed numbers*.

a)  _____

b) 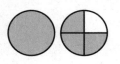 _____

c) 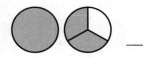 _____

d)  _____

e)  _____

f) 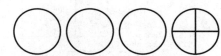 _____

g) _____

3. Shade the amount of pie given in the mixed number. There may be more pies than you need.

a) $3\frac{1}{2}$

b) $1\frac{1}{4}$

c) $2\frac{3}{4}$

d) $3\frac{2}{3}$

e) $1\frac{2}{5}$

f) $2\frac{5}{6}$

4. Sketch.

a) $2\frac{1}{3}$ pies

b) $3\frac{3}{4}$ pies

c) $2\frac{3}{5}$ pies

d) $4\frac{1}{2}$ pies

Jennifer and her friends ate 9 quarter-sized pieces of pizza.

Altogether they ate $\frac{9}{4}$ pizzas.

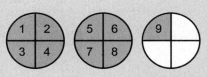

When the numerator of a fraction is larger than the denominator, the fraction represents *more than* a whole. Such fractions are called **improper fractions**.

**5.** Describe the shaded area as an *improper* fraction.

a)   _____

b) 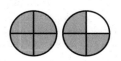 _____

c) 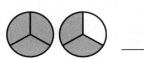 _____

d) 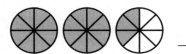 _____

e) 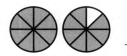 _____

f) 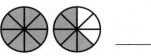 _____

g) 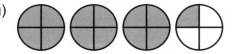 _____

h) 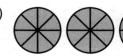 _____

**6.** Shade one piece at a time until you have shaded the given improper fraction.

a) $\frac{5}{2}$

b) $\frac{7}{4}$

c) $\frac{11}{3}$

d) $\frac{12}{4}$

e) $\frac{17}{5}$

f) $\frac{21}{8}$

g) $\frac{17}{6}$

h) $\frac{11}{5}$

**7.** Sketch.

a) $\frac{6}{4}$ pies

b) $\frac{7}{2}$ pies

c) $\frac{11}{4}$ pies

d) $\frac{13}{3}$ pies

**8.** Is the fraction more than a whole? How do you know?

a) $\frac{9}{10}$

b) $\frac{15}{7}$

c) $\frac{12}{8}$

# 26. Mixed Numbers and Improper Fractions

How many quarter pieces are in $2\frac{3}{4}$ pies?

4 quarters       8 ($= 2 \times 4$) quarters       8 quarters + 3 extra quarters = 11 quarters

So there are 11 quarters altogether in $2\frac{3}{4}$ pies.

1. Find the number of *halves* in the amount.

   a) 1 pie = _____ halves

   b) 2 pies = _____ halves

   c) 3 pies = _____ halves

   d) $2\frac{1}{2}$ pies = _____ halves

   e) $3\frac{1}{2}$ pies = _____ halves

   f) $4\frac{1}{2}$ pies = _____ halves

2. Find the number of *thirds* or *quarters* in the amount.

   a) 1 pie = _____ thirds

   b) 2 pies = _____ thirds

   c) 3 pies = _____ thirds

   d) $1\frac{2}{3}$ pies = _____ thirds

   e) $2\frac{1}{3}$ pies = _____ thirds

   f) $4\frac{2}{3}$ pies = _____ thirds

   g) 1 pie = _____ quarters

   h) 2 pies = _____ quarters

   i) 5 pies = _____ quarters

   j) $2\frac{3}{4}$ pies = _____ quarters

   k) $5\frac{1}{4}$ pies = _____ quarters

   l) $5\frac{3}{4}$ pies = _____ quarters

3. If 1 box holds 4 cans, ...

   a) 2 boxes hold _____ cans.

   b) 3 boxes hold _____ cans.

   c) 4 boxes hold _____ cans.

   d) $2\frac{1}{4}$ boxes hold _____ cans.

   e) $3\frac{1}{4}$ boxes hold _____ cans.

   f) $4\frac{3}{4}$ boxes hold _____ cans.

4. If 1 box holds 6 cans, ...

   a) $2\frac{1}{6}$ boxes hold _____ cans.

   b) $2\frac{5}{6}$ boxes hold _____ cans.

   c) $3\frac{1}{6}$ boxes hold _____ cans.

5. Pens come in packs of 6. Peter used $1\frac{5}{6}$ packs. How many pens did he use? _____

6. Jerome needs $4\frac{2}{3}$ cups of flour.

   a) Which scoop should he use? _____

   b) How many scoops will he need? _____

   A   $\frac{1}{3}$ cup

   B   $\frac{1}{4}$ cup

How many whole pies are there in $\frac{13}{4}$ pies?

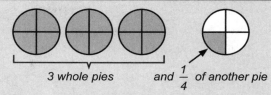

3 whole pies    and $\frac{1}{4}$ of another pie

There are 13 pieces altogether and each pie has 4 pieces.

So you can find the number of whole pies by dividing 13 by 4:    $13 \div 4 = 3$ Remainder 1

There are 3 whole pies and 1 quarter left over, so:      $\frac{13}{4} = 3\frac{1}{4}$

7. Find the number of whole pies in the amount by dividing.

a) $\frac{6}{2}$ pies = _____ whole pies    b) $\frac{15}{3}$ pies = _____ whole pies   c) $\frac{16}{4}$ pies = _____ whole pies

8. Find the number of whole pies and the number of pieces remaining by dividing.

a) $\frac{7}{2}$ pies = __3__ whole pies and __1__ half pie = $3\frac{1}{2}$ pies

b) $\frac{11}{3}$ pies = _____ whole pies and _____ thirds =    pies

c) $\frac{15}{4}$ pies = _____ whole pies and _____ =    pies

9. a) Write a mixed number and an improper fraction for the number of liters.

    b) Write a mixed number and an improper fraction for the length of the rope.

1 L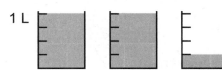

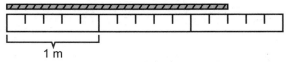

1 m

Mixed Number:    Improper Fraction:      Mixed Number:    Improper Fraction:

10. Write the improper fraction as a mixed number by dividing.

a) $\frac{9}{2}$                  b) $\frac{15}{4}$                c) $\frac{22}{5}$

   $9 \div 2 =$ _____ R _____      $15 \div 4 =$ _____ R _____      $22 \div 5 =$ _____ R _____

   So $\frac{9}{2} =$             So $\frac{15}{4} =$             So $\frac{22}{5} =$

d) $\frac{14}{5} =$    e) $\frac{68}{10} =$    f) $\frac{32}{3} =$    g) $\frac{28}{7} =$    h) $\frac{40}{7} =$    i) $\frac{30}{8} =$

11. Draw a picture to find out which fraction is greater.

a) $3\frac{1}{2}$   or   $\frac{5}{2}$            b) $2\frac{4}{5}$   or   $\frac{12}{5}$            c) $4\frac{1}{3}$   or   $\frac{14}{3}$

# 27. Adding and Subtracting Fractions (Introduction)

1. Imagine moving the shaded pieces from pies A and B onto pie plate C. Show how much of pie plate C would be filled and then write a fraction for pie C.

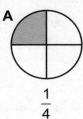  

A $\qquad$ B $\qquad$ C

$$\frac{1}{4} \qquad + \qquad \frac{2}{4} \qquad = $$

2. Imagine pouring the liquid from cups A and B into cup C. Shade the amount of liquid that would be in C. Then complete the addition statement

a)

$$\frac{3}{5} \quad + \quad \frac{}{5} \quad = \quad \underline{\quad}$$

b)

$$\frac{}{3} \quad + \quad \frac{}{3} \quad = \quad \underline{\quad}$$

3. Add.

a) $\frac{2}{5} + \frac{1}{5} =$     b) $\frac{1}{4} + \frac{1}{4} =$     c) $\frac{4}{7} + \frac{2}{7} =$     d) $\frac{4}{9} + \frac{1}{9} =$

e) $\frac{5}{13} + \frac{6}{13} =$     f) $\frac{7}{23} + \frac{11}{23} =$     g) $\frac{8}{25} + \frac{13}{25} =$     h) $\frac{19}{43} + \frac{18}{43} =$

4. Show how much pie would be left if you took away the amount shown. Then complete the subtraction statement.

a)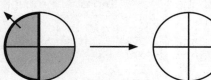

$$\frac{3}{4} - \frac{2}{4} \quad = \quad \underline{\quad}$$

b)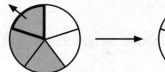

$$\frac{3}{5} - \frac{1}{5} \quad = \quad \underline{\quad}$$

5. Subtract.

a) $\frac{4}{7} - \frac{1}{7} =$     b) $\frac{2}{5} - \frac{1}{5} =$     c) $\frac{2}{3} - \frac{1}{3} =$     d) $\frac{7}{8} - \frac{5}{8} =$

e) $\frac{11}{13} - \frac{10}{13} =$     f) $\frac{7}{18} - \frac{2}{18} =$     g) $\frac{23}{27} - \frac{16}{27} =$     h) $\frac{31}{73} - \frac{11}{73} =$

# 28. Adding and Subtracting Mixed Numbers (Introduction)

1. How many halves are in the amount?

a) $4\frac{1}{2} + 1\frac{1}{2}$    $(4 \times 2) + 1$    $(1 \times 2) + 1$

$= \underline{\ 9\ }$ halves $+ \underline{\ 3\ }$ halves

$= \underline{\ 12\ }$ halves

b) $2\frac{1}{2} + 5\frac{1}{2}$

$= \underline{\ \ \ \ }$ halves $+ \underline{\ \ \ \ }$ halves

$= \underline{\ \ \ \ }$ halves

c) $5\frac{1}{2} - 3$

$= \underline{\ \ \ \ }$ halves $- \underline{\ \ \ \ }$ halves

$= \underline{\ \ \ \ }$ halves

d) $6 - 3\frac{1}{2}$

$= \underline{\ \ \ \ }$ halves $- \underline{\ \ \ \ }$ halves

$= \underline{\ \ \ \ }$ halves

2. How many thirds are in the amount?

a) $5\frac{1}{3} + 4\frac{1}{3}$

$= \underline{\ \ \ \ }$ thirds $+ \underline{\ \ \ \ }$ thirds

$= \underline{\ \ \ \ }$ thirds

b) $4\frac{2}{3} - 3\frac{1}{3}$

$= \underline{\ \ \ \ }$ thirds $- \underline{\ \ \ \ }$ thirds

$= \underline{\ \ \ \ }$ thirds

c) $5\frac{1}{3} + 1\frac{2}{3}$

$= \underline{\ \ \ \ }$ thirds $+ \underline{\ \ \ \ }$ thirds

$= \underline{\ \ \ \ }$ thirds

d) $6\frac{1}{3} - 2\frac{2}{3}$

$= \underline{\ \ \ \ }$ thirds $- \underline{\ \ \ \ }$ thirds

$= \underline{\ \ \ \ }$ thirds

3. Use the method from Questions 1 and 2 to add or subtract mixed numbers.

a) $3\frac{1}{4} - 1\frac{3}{4}$

b) $4\frac{2}{5} + 2\frac{1}{5}$

4. Kim needs $2\frac{1}{3}$ cups of flour to make bread and 3 cups of flour to make dumplings.

How much flour does she need altogether?

5. a) Bran bought a rope $3\frac{1}{2}$ feet long. He cut off $1\frac{1}{2}$ feet from it.

How much rope is left?

b) Lou bought $6\frac{1}{3}$ meters of ribbon. He used $1\frac{2}{3}$ meters to wrap Chu's gift and

2 meters to wrap Kathy's gift. How much ribbon is left?

# 29. Equivalent Fractions and Multiplication

1. Compare the pair of circles.

a) 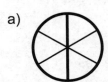 has _____ times as many parts as

b)  has _____ times as many parts as

c)  has _____ times as many parts as

d)  has _____ times as many parts as

2. Fill in the blanks.

a) A has _____ times as many parts as B.

   A has _____ times as many shaded parts as B.

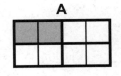

b) A has _____ times as many parts as B.

   A has _____ times as many shaded parts as B.

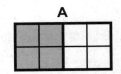 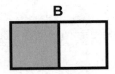

c) A has _____ times as many parts as B.

   A has _____ times as many shaded parts as B.

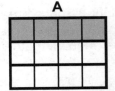 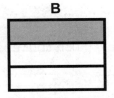

d) A has _____ times as many parts as B.

   A has _____ times as many shaded parts as B.

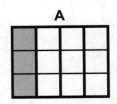 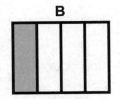

Equivalent fractions are fractions that have the same value or represent the same amount.

3. Write an equivalent fraction for the picture. Then write how many times the numerator and denominator are multiplied.

a)

$$\frac{1}{4} \xrightarrow[\times 2]{\times 2} = \frac{2}{8}$$

Equivalent fractions

b)

$$\frac{1}{3} \xrightarrow[\times]{\times} = \frac{\square}{\square}$$

c)
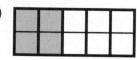

$$\frac{2}{5} \xrightarrow[\times]{\times} = \frac{\square}{\square}$$

d)
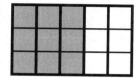

$$\frac{3}{5} \xrightarrow[\times]{\times} = \frac{\square}{\square}$$

e)
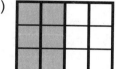

$$\frac{2}{4} \xrightarrow[\times]{\times} = \frac{\square}{\square}$$

f)

$$\frac{2}{3} \xrightarrow[\times]{\times} = \frac{\square}{\square}$$

g)
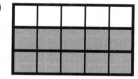

$$\frac{2}{3} \xrightarrow[\times]{\times} = \frac{\square}{\square}$$

h)
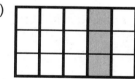

$$\frac{1}{5} \xrightarrow[\times]{\times} = \frac{\square}{\square}$$

i)

$$\frac{2}{4} \xrightarrow[\times]{\times} = \frac{\square}{\square}$$

BONUS ▶ Write two fractions to describe the portion shaded.

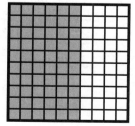

$$\frac{\square}{\square} \xrightarrow[\times]{\times} = \frac{\square}{\square}$$

You can multiply the numerator and denominator by the same number to get an equivalent fraction.

Example:  Picture A   $\dfrac{3}{4} \xrightarrow[\times 2]{\times 2} \dfrac{6}{8}$  Picture B

Picture B has twice as many **parts** as Picture A.
Picture B has twice as many **shaded parts** as Picture A.

4. Draw lines to cut the pies into more pieces. Then fill in the numerators of the equivalent fractions.

a)

    4 pieces     6 pieces     8 pieces

$\dfrac{1}{2} = \dfrac{}{4} = \dfrac{}{6} = \dfrac{}{8}$

b)

    6 pieces     9 pieces     12 pieces

$\dfrac{1}{3} = \dfrac{}{6} = \dfrac{}{9} = \dfrac{}{12}$

5. Cut the pie into more pieces. Then fill in the missing numbers.

a) 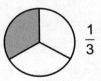 $\dfrac{1}{3} \xrightarrow[\times 2]{\times 2} \dfrac{}{6}$

This number tells you how many pieces to cut each slice into.

b)  $\dfrac{2}{4} \xrightarrow[\times 2]{\times 2} \dfrac{}{8}$

c) 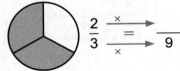 $\dfrac{2}{3} \xrightarrow[\times]{\times} \dfrac{}{9}$

6. Use multiplication to find the equivalent fraction.

a) $\dfrac{2}{3} \xrightarrow[\times 2]{\times 2} \dfrac{}{6}$     b) $\dfrac{1}{2} = \dfrac{}{10}$    c) $\dfrac{2}{5} = \dfrac{}{10}$    d) $\dfrac{1}{4} = \dfrac{}{20}$

e) $\dfrac{3}{4} = \dfrac{}{16}$    f) $\dfrac{3}{5} = \dfrac{}{15}$    g) $\dfrac{3}{10} = \dfrac{}{20}$    h) $\dfrac{4}{7} = \dfrac{}{35}$

7. Write five fractions equivalent to $\dfrac{3}{10}$.

$\dfrac{3}{10} = \boxed{\phantom{xx}} = \boxed{\phantom{xx}} = \boxed{\phantom{xx}} = \boxed{\phantom{xx}} = \boxed{\phantom{xx}}$

**JUMP Math Accumula**

# 30. Comparing Fractions Using Equivalent Fractions

1. Draw lines to cut the pies into more equal pieces. Then fill in the numerators of the equivalent fractions.

   a)

   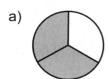   

   $$\frac{2}{3} = \frac{\phantom{0}}{6} = \frac{\phantom{0}}{9} = \frac{\phantom{0}}{12}$$

   b)

   $$\frac{3}{4} = \frac{\phantom{0}}{8} = \frac{\phantom{0}}{12} = \frac{\phantom{0}}{16}$$

2. a) Use your answers from Question 1. Write two fractions with the same denominators.

   $\frac{2}{3} = \boxed{\phantom{0}}$ and $\frac{3}{4} = \boxed{\phantom{0}}$

   b) Which of the two fractions is greater, $\frac{2}{3}$ or $\frac{3}{4}$? _____

   How do you know? _____

   _____

3. Write equivalent fractions with the same denominator. Then circle the larger fraction.

   a) $\frac{1}{4} = \frac{\phantom{0}}{20}$ and $\frac{3}{5} = \frac{\phantom{0}}{20}$    b) $\frac{2}{7} = \frac{\phantom{0}}{21}$ and $\frac{2}{3} = \frac{\phantom{0}}{21}$

4. a) Write an equivalent fraction with denominator 18.

   i) $\frac{1}{2} = \frac{\phantom{0}}{18}$    ii) $\frac{1}{6} = \frac{\phantom{0}}{18}$    iii) $\frac{5}{9} = \frac{\phantom{0}}{18}$    iv) $\frac{2}{3} = \frac{\phantom{0}}{18}$

   b) Write the fractions from part a) in order from least to greatest.

   $\boxed{\phantom{0}} < \boxed{\phantom{0}} < \boxed{\phantom{0}} < \boxed{\phantom{0}}$

5. Draw lines to cut the left-hand pie into the same number of pieces as the right-hand pie. Complete the equivalent fraction. Then circle the greater fraction.

a)

$\dfrac{1}{2} =$     $\dfrac{3}{4}$

b)

$\dfrac{2}{3} =$     $\dfrac{3}{6}$

---

To compare $\dfrac{1}{3}$ and $\dfrac{2}{5}$ you can change them into fractions with the same denominator.

*Multiply the numerator and denominator of the first fraction by the denominator of the second.*

*Multiply the numerator and denominator of the second fraction by the denominator of the first.*

$$\dfrac{5\times 1}{5\times 3} = \dfrac{5}{15} \qquad \dfrac{6}{15} = \dfrac{2\times 3}{5\times 3}$$

Now the fractions are easy to compare: $\dfrac{5}{15} < \dfrac{6}{15}$, so $\dfrac{1}{3} < \dfrac{2}{5}$

---

6. Compare the pairs of fractions. First, turn the fraction on the left into an equivalent fraction with the same denominator as the fraction on the right. Then write < (less than) or > (greater than) to show which fraction is greater.

a) $\dfrac{2\times 2}{3\times 2} = \dfrac{4}{6} \boxed{<} \dfrac{5}{6}$

b) $\dfrac{3}{4} = \dfrac{\phantom{0}}{8} \square \dfrac{5}{8}$

c) $\dfrac{1}{2} = \dfrac{\phantom{0}}{\phantom{0}} \square \dfrac{3}{4}$

d) $\dfrac{1}{2} = \dfrac{\phantom{0}}{\phantom{0}} \square \dfrac{4}{10}$

e) $\dfrac{1}{2} = \dfrac{\phantom{0}}{\phantom{0}} \square \dfrac{3}{12}$

f) $\dfrac{1}{3} = \dfrac{\phantom{0}}{\phantom{0}} \square \dfrac{4}{9}$

g) $\dfrac{5}{6} = \dfrac{\phantom{0}}{\phantom{0}} \square \dfrac{13}{18}$

h) $\dfrac{1}{5} = \dfrac{\phantom{0}}{\phantom{0}} \square \dfrac{4}{10}$

i) $\dfrac{1}{4} = \dfrac{\phantom{0}}{\phantom{0}} \square \dfrac{7}{16}$

7. Turn the fractions into fractions with the same denominator. Then compare with < or >.

a) $\dfrac{3\times 2}{3\times 5} \qquad \dfrac{1\times 5}{3\times 5}$

$= \dfrac{\phantom{0}}{15} \qquad = \dfrac{\phantom{0}}{15}$

so $\dfrac{2}{5} \square \dfrac{1}{3}$

b) $\dfrac{3}{4} \qquad \dfrac{2}{3}$

$= \dfrac{\phantom{0}}{\phantom{0}} \qquad = \dfrac{\phantom{0}}{\phantom{0}}$

so $\dfrac{3}{4} \square \dfrac{2}{3}$

c) $\dfrac{1}{2} \qquad \dfrac{2}{5}$

$= \dfrac{\phantom{0}}{\phantom{0}} \qquad = \dfrac{\phantom{0}}{\phantom{0}}$

so $\dfrac{1}{2} \square \dfrac{2}{5}$

d) $\dfrac{2}{3}$ and $\dfrac{5}{8}$

e) $\dfrac{2}{3}$ and $\dfrac{3}{5}$

f) $\dfrac{5}{17}$ and $\dfrac{3}{10}$

8. A turtle weighs $\dfrac{4}{9}$ kg and a lizard weighs $\dfrac{5}{11}$ kg. Which animal is heavier? Explain how you know.

# 31. Factors

There are only four ways to write 6 as a product of two whole numbers:

$1 \times 6 = 6$       $2 \times 3 = 6$       $3 \times 2 = 6$       $6 \times 1 = 6$

The numbers that appear in the products are called the **factors** of 6.

The factors of 6 are the numbers 1, 2, 3, and 6.

1. Write the number that makes the equation true. If no number makes the equation true, write "✕" in the box.

   a)  $2 \times \boxed{5} = 10$       b)  $3 \times \boxed{✕} = 14$       c)  $5 \times \boxed{\phantom{0}} = 12$       d)  $5 \times \boxed{\phantom{0}} = 10$

2. Write "yes" or "no." Use your answers to Question 1 to explain.

   a)  Is 2 a factor of 10? ___yes___ because ___5 makes the equation true___ .

   b)  Is 3 a factor of 14? ___no___ because ___no number makes the equation true___ .

   c)  Is 5 a factor of 12? _____ because _____ .

   d)  Is 5 a factor of 10? _____ because _____ .

3. Write the number that makes the equation true. If no number fits, write "✕" in the box. Then list the factors of the number.

   a)  Find the factors of 4.

   $1 \times \boxed{4} = 4$

   $2 \times \boxed{2} = 4$

   $3 \times \boxed{✕} = 4$

   $4 \times \boxed{1} = 4$

   The factors of 4 are

   ___1, 2, 4___

   b)  Find the factors of 6.

   $1 \times \boxed{\phantom{0}} = 6$

   $2 \times \boxed{\phantom{0}} = 6$

   $3 \times \boxed{\phantom{0}} = 6$

   $4 \times \boxed{\phantom{0}} = 6$

   $5 \times \boxed{\phantom{0}} = 6$

   $6 \times \boxed{\phantom{0}} = 6$

   The factors of 6 are

   _____

   c)  Find the factors of 8.

   $1 \times \boxed{\phantom{0}} = 8$

   $2 \times \boxed{\phantom{0}} = 8$

   $3 \times \boxed{\phantom{0}} = 8$

   $4 \times \boxed{\phantom{0}} = 8$

   $5 \times \boxed{\phantom{0}} = 8$

   $6 \times \boxed{\phantom{0}} = 8$

   $7 \times \boxed{\phantom{0}} = 8$

   $8 \times \boxed{\phantom{0}} = 8$

   The factors of 8 are

   _____

2 and 3 are a **factor pair** of 6 because $2 \times 3 = 6$.

4. List the factor pairs of the number. List each pair only once.

   a) 6

       __1__ and __6__

       __2__ and __3__

   b) 4

       _____ and _____

       _____ and _____

   c) 15

       _____ and _____

       _____ and _____

5. Mia lists the factor pairs of 10 by using a table. When a number is not a factor, she writes an "✘" in the second column.

   a) Why didn't Mia list 11 as a first factor?

       _____

   b) Use Mia's table to write the factors of 10.

       _____ , _____ , _____ , _____

   c) Use Mia's table to write the factor pairs of 10.

       _____ and _____      _____ and _____

| First Factor | Second Factor |
|---|---|
| 1 | 10 |
| 2 | 5 |
| 3 | ✘ |
| 4 | ✘ |
| 5 | 2 |
| 6 | ✘ |
| 7 | ✘ |
| 8 | ✘ |
| 9 | ✘ |
| 10 | 1 |

6. a) Use Mia's method to find all the factor pairs of 12.

| First Factor | Second Factor |
|---|---|
| 1 | |
| 2 | |
| 3 | |
| 4 | |
| 5 | |
| 6 | |
| 7 | |
| 8 | |
| 9 | |
| 10 | |
| 11 | |
| 12 | |

Factor pairs of 12:

    _____ and _____

    _____ and _____

    _____ and _____

b) Write "bigger" or "smaller" in the blanks:

As you go down the table, the first factor gets

_____ and the second factor gets _____ .

7. Use Mia's method to find all the factor pairs of the number.

    a) 8      b) 9      c) 14      d) 15      e) 18      f) 20      g) 24

# 32. Factors and Common Factors

> **REMINDER ▶** You can write a division statement with remainder 0 for every multiplication.
>
> Example: $2 \times 7 = 14$, so $14 \div 2 = 7$ R 0

1. Write a division equation with remainder 0 for the multiplication equation.

   a) $4 \times 3 = 12$ so ___$12 \div 4 = 3\,R\,0$___

   b) $7 \times 4 = 28$ so _____

   c) $3 \times 6 = 18$ so _____

   d) $3 \times 4 = 12$ so _____

You can use division to check for factors.

Example: 3 is a factor of 6 because $6 \div 3$ has remainder 0.

2. Use division to answer the question.

   a) $16 \div 8 =$ _____ R _____

   Is 8 a factor of 16? _____

   b) $14 \div 5 =$ _____ R _____

   Is 5 a factor of 14? _____

   c) $34 \div 4 =$ _____ R _____

   Is 4 a factor of 34? _____

   d) $24 \div 3 =$ _____ R _____

   Is 3 a factor of 24? _____

   e) $63 \div 7 =$ _____ R _____

   Is 7 a factor of 63? _____

   f) $54 \div 8 =$ _____ R _____

   Is 8 a factor of 54? _____

To list all the factors of a given number, stop when you get a number that is already part of a factor pair.

3. Complete the table to find all the factor pairs. There might be more rows than you need.

a) 20

| First Factor | Second Factor |
|---|---|
| 1 | 20 |
| 2 | 10 |
| 4 | 5 |
| 5 | |

b) 64

| First Factor | Second Factor |
|---|---|
| 1 | 64 |
| 2 | 32 |
| 4 | 16 |
| 8 | 8 |

c) 34

| First Factor | Second Factor |
|---|---|
| | |
| | |
| | |
| | |

d) 24

| First Factor | Second Factor |
|---|---|
| | |
| | |
| | |
| | |

e) 30

| First Factor | Second Factor |
|---|---|
| | |
| | |
| | |
| | |

f) 66

| First Factor | Second Factor |
|---|---|
| | |
| | |
| | |
| | |

4.  List all the factors for the number. Use division to determine the factors. Hint: Divide by 1, then 2, then 3, and so on. If the remainder of division is 0, then the number is a factor.

a) 10: ___*1, 2, 5, 10*___       b) 7: ___*1, 7*___

c) 4: _____       d) 6: _____

e) 9: _____       f) 8: _____

g) 5: _____       h) 12: _____

i) 15: _____       j) 18: _____

---

2 is a **common factor** of 4 and 10 because it is a factor of both numbers.

---

5.  Write "yes" or "no." Use your answers to Question 4 to explain.

a) Is 2 a common factor of 7 and 10? __*no*__ because __*2 is a factor of 10, but not a factor of 7*__.

b) Is 1 a common factor of 7 and 10? __*yes*__ because __*1 is a factor of both 7 and 10*__.

c) Is 3 a common factor of 6 and 9? _____ because _____.

d) Is 2 a common factor of 6 and 12? _____ because _____.

e) Is 5 a common factor of 5 and 10? _____ because _____.

f) Is 6 a common factor of 12 and 15? _____ because _____.

6.  Use your answers to Question 4 to write all common factors of the two numbers.

a) 4 and 10: ___*1, 2*___       b) 6 and 8: _____

c) 6 and 9: _____       d) 5 and 7: _____

e) 5 and 10: _____       f) 4 and 9: _____

g) 6 and 12: _____       h) 9 and 12: _____

i) 9 and 15: _____       j) 12 and 18: _____

7.  A child is arranging green blocks in groups of 4 and purple blocks in groups of 6. She has the same number of green and purple blocks. What is the smallest number of each color that she could have?

8.  Blanca and Jerry are training for a marathon. Blanca runs 15 km at a time while Jerry prefers to run in blocks of 8 km. At the end of a month, they realize that they have run the same total number of kilometers. What is the smallest number of kilometers that each must have run?

# 33. Flexibility with Equivalent Fractions and Lowest Terms

**1.** Group the squares to show ...

a) six twelfths equals one half $\left(\dfrac{6}{12} = \dfrac{1}{2}\right)$

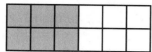

b) six twelfths equals three sixths $\left(\dfrac{6}{12} = \dfrac{3}{6}\right)$

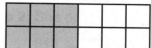

**2.** Group shaded squares to show an equivalent fraction.

a)

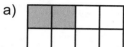

$$\dfrac{2}{8} = \dfrac{}{4}$$

b)

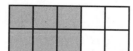

$$\dfrac{6}{10} = \dfrac{}{5}$$

c)

$$\dfrac{3}{9} = \dfrac{}{3}$$

**3.** Imagine erasing the dotted lines in the first circle. Shade the second circle to show the result and then write the equivalent fraction.

a)

$$\dfrac{2}{4}$$  $\boxed{\dfrac{1}{2}}$

b)

$$\dfrac{2}{6}$$

c)

$$\dfrac{4}{8}$$

d)

$$\dfrac{4}{8}$$

e)

$$\dfrac{4}{6}$$

f)

$$\dfrac{6}{9}$$

**4.** Imagine erasing the dotted lines. Then write the equivalent fraction.

a)  $\dfrac{4}{6} \xrightarrow[\div 2]{\div 2} = \dfrac{\phantom{0}}{3}$

This number tells you how many slices to combine

b) 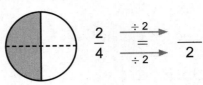 $\dfrac{2}{4} \xrightarrow[\div 2]{\div 2} = \dfrac{\phantom{0}}{2}$

c)  $\dfrac{2}{8} \xrightarrow[\div 2]{\div 2} = \dfrac{\phantom{0}}{\phantom{0}}$

d)  $\dfrac{4}{8} \xrightarrow[\div 4]{\div 4} = \dfrac{\phantom{0}}{\phantom{0}}$

e)  $\dfrac{3}{9} \xrightarrow[\div 3]{\div 3} = \dfrac{\phantom{0}}{\phantom{0}}$

f)  $\dfrac{4}{10} \xrightarrow[\div 2]{\div 2} = \dfrac{\phantom{0}}{\phantom{0}}$

---

You can divide the numerator and denominator by the same number to get an equivalent fraction.

Example:  Picture A                          Picture B

   $\dfrac{2}{4} \xrightarrow[\div 2]{\div 2} = \dfrac{1}{2}$

Picture A has twice as many **parts** as Picture B.
Picture A has twice as many **shaded parts** as Picture B.

---

**5.** Use division to find the equivalent fractions.

a) $\dfrac{2}{6} \xrightarrow[\div 2]{\div 2} = \dfrac{\phantom{0}}{3}$

b) $\dfrac{5}{10} \xrightarrow[\div 5]{\div 5} = \dfrac{\phantom{0}}{2}$

c) $\dfrac{2}{10} \xrightarrow[\div 2]{\div 2} = \dfrac{1}{\phantom{0}}$

d) $\dfrac{3}{6} \xrightarrow[\div 3]{\div 3} = \dfrac{1}{\phantom{0}}$

e) $\dfrac{10}{15} \xrightarrow[\div 5]{\div 5} = \dfrac{\phantom{0}}{3}$

f) $\dfrac{8}{28} \xrightarrow[\div 4]{\div 4} = \dfrac{2}{\phantom{0}}$

**6.** Use division to write three fractions equivalent to …

a) $\dfrac{8}{32} = \boxed{\phantom{00}} = \boxed{\phantom{00}} = \boxed{\phantom{00}}$

b) $\dfrac{27}{54} = \boxed{\phantom{00}} = \boxed{\phantom{00}} = \boxed{\phantom{00}}$

c) $\dfrac{12}{36} = \boxed{\phantom{00}} = \boxed{\phantom{00}} = \boxed{\phantom{00}}$

d) $\dfrac{30}{60} = \boxed{\phantom{00}} = \boxed{\phantom{00}} = \boxed{\phantom{00}}$

A fraction is reduced to **lowest terms** if the numerator and the denominator don't have any common factor greater than 1.

Example: $\frac{3}{6}$ is *not* in lowest terms (because the common factor of 3 and 6 is 3)

but $\frac{1}{2}$ is lowest term.

To reduce a fraction to lowest terms, divide the numerator and the denominator by their common factor.

$$\frac{3}{6} \xrightarrow[\div 3]{\div 3} = \frac{1}{2}$$

**7.** Complete the division to reduce the fraction.

a) $\frac{2}{4} \xrightarrow[\div 2]{\div 2} = \frac{1}{2}$

b) $\frac{2}{6} \xrightarrow[\div 2]{\div 2} = \underline{\quad}$

c) $\frac{4}{8} \xrightarrow[\div 4]{\div 4} = \underline{\quad}$

d) $\frac{3}{9} \xrightarrow[\div 3]{\div 3} = \underline{\quad}$

e) $\frac{6}{8} \xrightarrow[\div 2]{\div 2} = \underline{\quad}$

f) $\frac{2}{10} \xrightarrow[\div 2]{\div 2} = \underline{\quad}$

g) $\frac{5}{15} \xrightarrow[\div 5]{\div 5} = \underline{\quad}$

h) $\frac{8}{12} \xrightarrow[\div 4]{\div 4} = \underline{\quad}$

i) $\frac{12}{15} \xrightarrow[\div 3]{\div 3} = \underline{\quad}$

j) $\frac{12}{18} \xrightarrow[\div 6]{\div 6} = \underline{\quad}$

k) $\frac{6}{21} \xrightarrow[\div 3]{\div 3} = \underline{\quad}$

l) $\frac{21}{28} \xrightarrow[\div 7]{\div 7} = \underline{\quad}$

**8.** Reduce the fraction by dividing.

a) $\frac{2}{10} = \underline{\quad}$

b) $\frac{3}{6} = \underline{\quad}$

c) $\frac{2}{8} = \underline{\quad}$

d) $\frac{2}{12} = \underline{\quad}$

e) $\frac{5}{15} = \underline{\quad}$

f) $\frac{3}{15} = \underline{\quad}$

g) $\frac{4}{12} = \underline{\quad}$

h) $\frac{6}{9} = \underline{\quad}$

i) $\frac{4}{6} = \underline{\quad}$

j) $\frac{10}{15} = \underline{\quad}$

k) $\frac{20}{25} = \underline{\quad}$

l) $\frac{9}{12} = \underline{\quad}$

m) $\frac{15}{18} = \underline{\quad}$

n) $\frac{28}{35} = \underline{\quad}$

o) $\frac{10}{15} = \underline{\quad}$

p) $\frac{21}{30} = \underline{\quad}$

**9.** Write whether the fraction is in lowest terms. Explain how you know.

a) $\frac{2}{11}$

b) $\frac{12}{27}$

c) $\frac{16}{25}$

d) $\frac{9}{33}$

**10.** Shondra says she reduced $\frac{12}{18}$ to lowest terms by dividing the numerator and denominator by 2.

$\frac{12}{18} \xrightarrow[\div 2]{\div 2} = \frac{6}{9}$ What mistake did she make? Explain.

# 34. Adding and Subtracting Fractions I

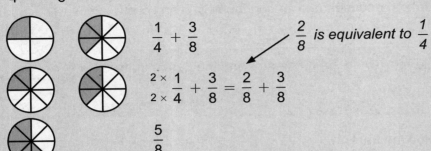

To add $\frac{1}{4}$ and $\frac{3}{8}$ Leila finds a fraction equivalent to $\frac{1}{4}$ with the denominator 8.

$\frac{1}{4} + \frac{3}{8}$

$\frac{2}{8}$ is equivalent to $\frac{1}{4}$

$\frac{2 \times 1}{2 \times 4} + \frac{3}{8} = \frac{2}{8} + \frac{3}{8}$

$\frac{5}{8}$

1. Add or subtract fractions by changing to equivalent fractions with the same denominator.

a) $\frac{2 \times 1}{2 \times 5} + \frac{7}{10}$

$= \frac{2}{10} + \frac{7}{10}$

$= \frac{9}{10}$

b) $\frac{1}{2} + \frac{1}{4}$

$=$

$=$

c) $\frac{7}{12} - \frac{1}{6}$

$=$

$=$

d) $\frac{1}{6} + \frac{11}{24}$

e) $\frac{5}{28} - \frac{1}{7}$

f) $\frac{4}{15} + \frac{2}{3}$

g) $\frac{3}{5} - \frac{3}{10}$

h) $\frac{1}{4} + \frac{5}{16}$

i) $\frac{2}{3} - \frac{1}{12}$

2. Saul walks $\frac{2}{3}$ mi from his home to his school. Rita walks $\frac{5}{6}$ mi from her home to school. How much farther does Rita walk to school than Saul?

3. A pastry stand has three kinds of pastries. Last week, $\frac{1}{4}$ of the pastries sold were meat pastries, $\frac{1}{2}$ were vegetable pastries, and $\frac{1}{8}$ were cheese pastries.

a) What fraction of the total number of pastries was sold?

b) What fraction was not sold?

# 35. Adding and Subtracting Fractions II

1. Make equivalent fractions for the pair of fractions until you find two with the same denominator.

a) $\dfrac{1}{3} = \dfrac{2}{6} = \dfrac{}{9} = \dfrac{}{12} = \dfrac{}{15}$

$\dfrac{2}{5} = \dfrac{}{10} = \dfrac{}{15}$

b) $\dfrac{2}{5} = \dfrac{}{10} = \dfrac{}{15} = \dfrac{}{20}$

$\dfrac{3}{4} = \dfrac{}{8} = \dfrac{}{12} = \dfrac{}{16} = \dfrac{}{20}$

c) $\dfrac{1}{4} = \dfrac{}{8} = \dfrac{}{12} = \dfrac{}{16} = \dfrac{}{20} = \dfrac{}{24} = \dfrac{}{28}$

$\dfrac{2}{7} = \dfrac{}{14} = \dfrac{}{21} = \dfrac{}{28}$

d) $\dfrac{5}{6} = \dfrac{}{12} = \dfrac{}{18} = \dfrac{}{24}$

$\dfrac{5}{8} = \dfrac{}{16} = \dfrac{}{24}$

---

Sam wants to add $\dfrac{1}{2} + \dfrac{2}{3}$.

He uses a diagram to create equivalent fractions with the same denominator.

$\dfrac{1}{2} = \dfrac{3}{6}$  and  $\dfrac{2}{3} = \dfrac{4}{6}$,  so the common denominator is 6.

Now he can add $\dfrac{1}{2} + \dfrac{2}{3} = \dfrac{3}{6} + \dfrac{4}{6} = \dfrac{7}{6}$

---

2. Use the pictures to add the fractions.

a)   $\dfrac{1}{2} = \dfrac{3}{6}$     $\dfrac{1}{2} + \dfrac{1}{3}$

  $\dfrac{1}{3} = \dfrac{2}{6}$     $= \dfrac{3}{6} + \dfrac{2}{6}$

$= \dfrac{5}{6}$

b)   $\dfrac{1}{2} = \dfrac{5}{10}$     $\dfrac{1}{2} + \dfrac{1}{5}$

  $\dfrac{1}{5} = \dfrac{2}{10}$     $=$

$=$

c)   $\dfrac{1}{2} = \text{---}$     $\dfrac{1}{2} + \dfrac{1}{4}$

  $\dfrac{1}{4} = \text{---}$     $=$     $=$

d)   $\dfrac{2}{3} = \text{---}$     $\dfrac{2}{3} + \dfrac{1}{6}$

  $\dfrac{1}{6} = \text{---}$     $=$     $=$

---

**JUMP Math Accumula**

73

Two fractions must have the same denominator (or a common denominator) to be added.
Remember, to create a common denominator:

*Multiply the numerator and denominator of the first fraction by the denominator of the second.*

*Multiply the numerator and denominator of the second fraction by the denominator of the first*

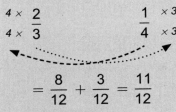

$$= \frac{8}{12} + \frac{3}{12} = \frac{11}{12}$$

3. Add the fractions by finding a common denominator.

a) $\frac{3 \times 1}{3 \times 2} + \frac{2 \times 2}{3 \times 2}$

$= \frac{3}{6} + \frac{4}{6} = \frac{7}{6}$

b) $\frac{3}{4} + \frac{2}{5}$

$=$

c) $\frac{3}{4} + \frac{2}{3}$

$=$

d) $\frac{3}{7} + \frac{1}{3}$

$=$

e) $\frac{1}{8} + \frac{1}{7}$

$=$

f) $\frac{2}{5} + \frac{1}{6}$

$=$

When the denominator of one fraction divides the denominator of another, you only need to change one fraction.

$\frac{5 \times 1}{5 \times 3} + \frac{2}{15}$

Change one fraction.

$\frac{7 \times 2}{7 \times 5} + \frac{3 \times 5}{7 \times 5}$

Change both.

4. Circle the pairs of fractions in which the denominator of one fraction divides into the other.

$\frac{1}{2} + \frac{3}{10}$        $\frac{1}{2} + \frac{2}{7}$        $\frac{4}{5} + \frac{9}{10}$        $\frac{2}{3} + \frac{5}{6}$        $\frac{3}{5} + \frac{5}{8}$        $\frac{3}{4} + \frac{11}{32}$

5. Add or subtract the fractions by changing them to equivalent fractions with the same denominator.

a) $\frac{2}{5} + \frac{1}{4}$

$=$

$=$

b) $\frac{4}{15} + \frac{2}{3}$

$=$

$=$

c) $\frac{2}{3} - \frac{1}{8}$

$=$

$=$

d) $\frac{3}{4} + \frac{1}{8}$

e) $\frac{11}{24} - \frac{1}{6}$

f) $\frac{2}{7} + \frac{1}{8}$

# 36. Adding and Subtracting Fractions Using the LCM

**Whole numbers** are the numbers 0, 1, 2, 3, and so on. The **multiples** of a whole number are the numbers you get by multiplying the number by another whole number. Examples:

The multiples of 2 are $2 \times 0 = 0$   $2 \times 1 = 2$   $2 \times 2 = 4$   $2 \times 3 = 6$   $2 \times 4 = 8$   ...

The multiples of 3 are $3 \times 0 = 0$   $3 \times 1 = 3$   $3 \times 2 = 6$   $3 \times 3 = 9$   $3 \times 4 = 12$   ...

**1.** a) Skip count to write the multiples of 3 up to $3 \times 10$.

  _0_ , _3_ , _6_ , _____ , _____ , _____ , _____ , _____ , _____ , _____ , _____

  b) Use your answers in part a) to circle the multiples of 3.

  12   17   22   24   25   27

A number is a **common multiple** of two numbers if it is a multiple of both of them.

**2.** List the multiples of both numbers, up to 10 times each number. Write the first two common multiples, not including 0.

  a) 3 and 5

  Multiples of 3: _0, 3, 6, 9, 12, 15, 18, 21, 24, 27, 30_____

  Multiples of 5: _____

  The first two common multiples are _____ and _____.

  b) 3 and 4

  Multiples of 3: _____

  Multiples of 4: _____

  The first two common multiples are _____ and _____.

  c) 2 and 5        d) 3 and 6        e) 2 and 7        f) 4 and 5

The number 0 is a multiple of every number. The **lowest common multiple (LCM)** of two numbers is the smallest whole number (not 0) that is a multiple of both numbers.

**3.** Find the lowest common multiple of the pair of numbers.

  a) 4 and 10                b) 5 and 10               c) 4 and 6

  4: _4, 8, 12, 16, 20_               5:                        4:

  10: _10, 20_                    10:                    6:

  LCM = _____              LCM = _____            LCM = _____

  d) 4 and 8                e) 9 and 12               f) 4 and 9

To add fractions with different denominators:

**Step 1:** Find the lowest common multiple (LCM) of the denominators.

$\dfrac{1}{3} + \dfrac{2}{5}$   Multiples of 3: 0, 3, 6, 9, 12, **15**, 18
Multiples of 5: 0, 5, 10, **15**, 20, 25, 30    The LCM of 3 and 5 is 15.

**Step 2:** Create equivalent fractions with the LCM as the denominator.

$$\dfrac{1}{3} + \dfrac{2}{5} = \dfrac{5\times\,1}{5\times\,3} + \dfrac{2}{5}\,{}^{\times\,3}_{\times\,3}$$

$$= \dfrac{5}{15} + \dfrac{6}{15}$$

$$= \dfrac{11}{15}$$

The LCM of the denominators is called the **lowest common denominator (LCD)** of the fractions.

4. Find the LCD of the pair of fractions. Then show what numbers you would multiply the numerator and denominator of each fraction by in order to add the fractions.

a) LCD = ___6___

$\dfrac{3\times\,1}{3\times\,2} + \dfrac{2}{3}\,{}^{\times\,2}_{\times\,2}$

b) LCD = _____

$\dfrac{3}{4} + \dfrac{1}{8}$

c) LCD = _____

$\dfrac{1}{20} + \dfrac{1}{5}$

d) LCD = _____

$\dfrac{3}{4} + \dfrac{2}{3}$

e) LCD = _____

$\dfrac{3}{7} + \dfrac{1}{3}$

f) LCD = _____

$\dfrac{1}{4} + \dfrac{1}{6}$

g) LCD = _____

$\dfrac{2}{5} + \dfrac{1}{10}$

h) LCD = _____

$\dfrac{1}{8} + \dfrac{1}{7}$

5. Add or subtract the fractions. First change them to equivalent fractions with denominators equal to the LCD of the fractions.

a) $\dfrac{1}{5} + \dfrac{3}{4}$

b) $\dfrac{1}{3} - \dfrac{2}{15}$

c) $\dfrac{2}{3} + \dfrac{1}{8}$

d) $\dfrac{2}{3} - \dfrac{1}{12}$

=

=

=

e) $\dfrac{3}{4} + \dfrac{1}{9}$

f) $\dfrac{5}{6} - \dfrac{2}{5}$

g) $\dfrac{5}{28} - \dfrac{1}{7}$

h) $\dfrac{2}{7} + \dfrac{5}{8}$

6. Add or subtract.

a) $\dfrac{1}{6} + \dfrac{5}{12}$

b) $\dfrac{17}{25} - \dfrac{3}{5}$

c) $\dfrac{6}{7} - \dfrac{1}{4}$

d) $\dfrac{4}{9} + \dfrac{2}{5}$

e) $\dfrac{2}{3} + \dfrac{1}{4} + \dfrac{1}{2}$

f) $\dfrac{3}{15} + \dfrac{2}{3} + \dfrac{1}{5}$

g) $\dfrac{7}{15} + \dfrac{1}{3} - \dfrac{3}{5}$

h) $\dfrac{1}{4} + \dfrac{17}{20} - \dfrac{3}{5}$

**JUMP Math Accumula**

# 37. Adding and Subtracting Mixed Numbers (Advanced)

$$1 + 2\frac{5}{6} = 3\frac{5}{6}$$
$$1 + 2$$

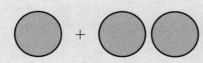  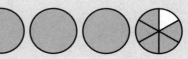

**1.** Add. Write your answer as a mixed number.

a) $3 + 6\frac{2}{5} =$

b) $1 + 4\frac{2}{3} =$

c) $5 + 3\frac{1}{2} =$

d) $3\frac{1}{3} + 4 =$

e) $4 + 2\frac{1}{4} =$

f) $2\frac{3}{5} + 1 =$

**2.** Add by adding the parts and the wholes separately.

a) $3\frac{1}{5} + 2\frac{3}{5} = 5\frac{4}{5}$

b) $3\frac{1}{3} + 1\frac{1}{3} =$

c) $2\frac{1}{7} + 3\frac{5}{7} =$

d) $4\frac{1}{6} + 2\frac{3}{6} =$

e) $2\frac{3}{8} + 4\frac{1}{8} =$

**BONUS ▶** $3\frac{2}{9} + 1\frac{3}{9} + 4\frac{1}{9} =$

---

Remember: A mixed number is made up of a whole number and a proper fraction.

When you add mixed numbers, the fraction part of the sum is sometimes an improper fraction (greater than 1).

Example: $1\frac{3}{6} + 2\frac{4}{6} = 3\frac{7}{6}$ ← $\frac{7}{6} > 1$

You can change the fraction part to a proper fraction.

Example: $3\frac{7}{6} = 3 + 1\frac{1}{6} = 4\frac{1}{6}$

---

**3.** Change the improper fraction to a mixed number.

a) $\frac{7}{5} = 1\frac{}{5}$

b) $\frac{3}{2} = 1\frac{}{2}$

c) $\frac{9}{7} = 1\frac{}{7}$

d) $\frac{6}{5} =$

e) $\frac{14}{10} =$

f) $\frac{8}{5} =$

g) $\frac{11}{6} =$

**BONUS ▶** $\frac{467}{462} =$

**4.** The mixed number includes an improper fraction. Change it so it includes a proper fraction.

a) $2\frac{4}{3} = 2 + 1\frac{1}{3} = 3\frac{1}{3}$

b) $6\frac{7}{5} =$

c) $4\frac{9}{8} =$

d) $3\frac{8}{6} =$

e) $5\frac{3}{2} =$

f) $8\frac{12}{7} =$

g) $7\frac{5}{3} =$

h) $2\frac{5}{4} =$

i) $3\frac{15}{9} =$

**5.** Add. You will need to change the fraction part of the sum to a proper fraction.

a) $3\frac{4}{7} + 2\frac{5}{7} = 5\frac{9}{7} = 5 + 1\frac{2}{7}$

$= 6\frac{2}{7}$

b) $4\frac{2}{3} + 1\frac{2}{3}$

c) $7\frac{4}{5} + 1\frac{3}{5}$

**6.** Make the mixed numbers have the same denominator. Add the wholes and the parts separately.

a) $2\frac{2}{7} + 4\frac{1}{2}$

$= 2\frac{4}{14} + 4\frac{7}{14} = 6\frac{11}{14}$

b) $5\frac{1}{3} + 4\frac{1}{2}$

c) $3\frac{2}{5} + 4\frac{1}{3}$

**7.** Add. You will need to change the fraction part of the sum to a proper fraction.

a) $3\frac{2}{5} + 1\frac{2}{3}$

b) $2\frac{3}{4} + 1\frac{1}{3}$

c) $4\frac{5}{6} + 2\frac{1}{5}$

**8.** Add. Write your answer in lowest terms.

a) $3\frac{3}{5} + 2\frac{9}{10}$

b) $3\frac{5}{6} + 4\frac{1}{4}$

c) $2\frac{1}{6} + 4\frac{8}{15}$

**9.** Subtract.

a) $2\frac{1}{2} - 1\frac{1}{2} = 1$

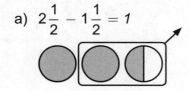

b) $3\frac{1}{4} - 2\frac{1}{4} =$

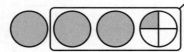

c) $3\frac{3}{4} - \frac{3}{4} =$

d) $2\frac{3}{4} - 1\frac{1}{4} = 1\frac{2}{4}$

e) $3\frac{5}{8} - 1\frac{2}{8} =$

f) $3\frac{7}{8} - 2 =$

**10.** Subtract by separating the wholes and the parts.

a) $5\frac{3}{7} - 3\frac{1}{7} = 2\frac{2}{7}$

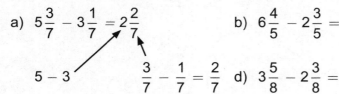

$5 - 3 \qquad \frac{3}{7} - \frac{1}{7} = \frac{2}{7}$

b) $6\frac{4}{5} - 2\frac{3}{5} =$

c) $6\frac{5}{9} - 3\frac{4}{9} =$

d) $3\frac{5}{8} - 2\frac{3}{8} =$

e) $4\frac{5}{11} - 1\frac{2}{11} =$

To subtract $9\frac{1}{4} - 5\frac{3}{4}$,

**Step 1:** Regroup $9\frac{1}{4}$ by subtracting 1 from 9 and adding 1 to $\frac{1}{4}$: $\quad 9\frac{1}{4} = 8 + 1\frac{1}{4} = 8\frac{5}{4}$

**Step 2:** Now you can subtract the wholes and parts separately: $\quad 9\frac{1}{4} - 5\frac{3}{4} = 8\frac{5}{4} - 5\frac{3}{4} = 3\frac{2}{4}$

11. Regroup the mixed number by subtracting 1 from the whole number and making an improper fraction.

a) $4\frac{2}{5} = 3\dfrac{\boxed{7}}{\boxed{5}}$

b) $3\frac{3}{4} = 2\dfrac{\boxed{\phantom{0}}}{\boxed{\phantom{0}}}$

c) $2\frac{3}{8} = 1\dfrac{\boxed{\phantom{0}}}{\boxed{\phantom{0}}}$

d) $4\frac{3}{7} =$

e) $2\frac{3}{5} =$

f) $4\frac{7}{11} =$

12. Subtract by regrouping.

a) $6\frac{1}{3} - 2\frac{2}{3} = 5\frac{4}{3} - 2\frac{2}{3}$
$\quad\quad = 3\frac{2}{3}$

b) $4\frac{1}{3} - 1\frac{2}{3}$

d) $6\frac{3}{5} - 2\frac{4}{5}$

c) $3\frac{5}{9} - 1\frac{7}{9}$

e) $4 - 2\frac{1}{2}$

13. Make the mixed numbers have the same denominator. Then subtract the wholes and the parts separately.

a) $5\frac{2}{3} - 3\frac{1}{2} = 5\frac{4}{6} - 3\frac{3}{6}$
$\quad\quad = 2\frac{1}{6}$

b) $6\frac{2}{5} - 1\frac{1}{3}$

d) $5\frac{4}{7} - 3\frac{1}{2}$

c) $4\frac{2}{3} - 2\frac{1}{4}$

e) $7\frac{5}{6} - 3\frac{2}{3}$

14. Subtract. You will need to regroup.

a) $3\frac{1}{5} - 1\frac{3}{4} = 2\frac{6}{5} - 1\frac{3}{4}$
$\quad\quad = 2\frac{24}{20} - 1\frac{15}{20}$
$\quad\quad = 1\frac{9}{20}$

b) $5\frac{3}{7} - 1\frac{1}{2} =$

c) $6\frac{3}{5} - 2\frac{2}{3} =$

15. Add or subtract. Write your answer in lowest terms.

a) $4\frac{1}{3} - 1\frac{1}{2}$

b) $2\frac{1}{5} + 3\frac{6}{7}$

c) $7\frac{1}{3} - 4\frac{2}{5}$

16. Tom cut $1\frac{2}{3}$ m from a 4 m rope. How much is left?

17. Each large loaf of banana bread is cut in 8 pieces. From 3 large loaves at Jennifer's birthday party, just $\frac{5}{8}$ of one is left. How much banana bread was eaten?

# 38. Fractions of Whole Numbers

Nick has 6 muffins. He wants to give $\frac{2}{3}$ of his muffins to his friends.

To do so, he shares the muffins equally onto 3 plates:

There are 3 equal groups, so each group is $\frac{1}{3}$ of 6.

There are 2 muffins in each group, so $\frac{1}{3}$ of 6 is 2.

There are 4 muffins in two groups, so $\frac{2}{3}$ of 6 is 4.

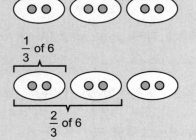

1. Use the picture to find the fraction of the number.

   a)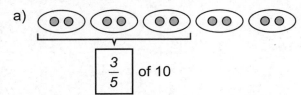
      $\boxed{\dfrac{3}{5}}$ of 10

   b)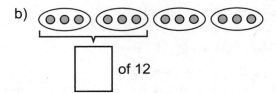
      $\boxed{\phantom{x}}$ of 12

2. Fill in the missing numbers.

   a)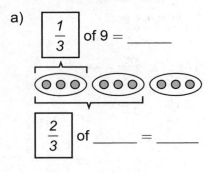
      $\boxed{\dfrac{1}{3}}$ of 9 = _____

      $\boxed{\dfrac{2}{3}}$ of _____ = _____

   b)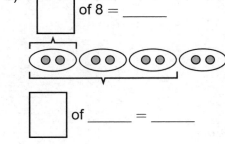
      $\boxed{\phantom{x}}$ of 8 = _____

      $\boxed{\phantom{x}}$ of _____ = _____

   c)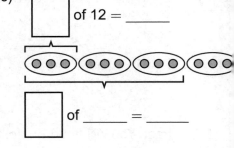
      $\boxed{\phantom{x}}$ of 12 = _____

      $\boxed{\phantom{x}}$ of _____ = _____

   d)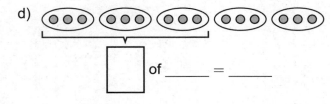
      $\boxed{\phantom{x}}$ of _____ = _____

   e)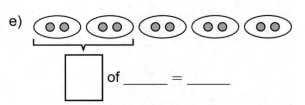
      $\boxed{\phantom{x}}$ of _____ = _____

3. Circle the given amount.

   a) $\frac{2}{3}$ of 9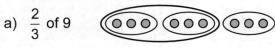

   b) $\frac{1}{5}$ of 10

   c) $\frac{3}{4}$ of 8

   d) $\frac{4}{5}$ of 15

**4.** Draw the correct number of dots in each group, then circle the given amount.

a) $\frac{2}{3}$ of 12

b) $\frac{2}{3}$ of 15

**5.** Find the fraction of the whole amount by sharing the food equally. Hint: Draw the correct number of plates and place the items one at a time. Then circle the correct amount.

a) Find $\frac{1}{4}$ of 8 apples.

$\frac{1}{4}$ of 8 is _____

b) Find $\frac{1}{2}$ of 10 muffins.

$\frac{1}{2}$ of 10 is _____

c) Find $\frac{2}{3}$ of 6 apples.

$\frac{2}{3}$ of 6 is _____

d) Find $\frac{3}{4}$ of 12 muffins.

$\frac{3}{4}$ of 12 is _____

Keesha finds $\frac{2}{3}$ of 15 as follows:

**Step 1:** She finds $\frac{1}{3}$ of 15 by dividing 15 by 3.

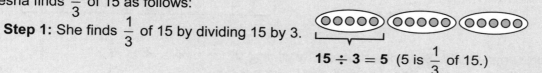

$15 \div 3 = 5$  (5 is $\frac{1}{3}$ of 15.)

**Step 2:** Then she multiplies the result by 2.

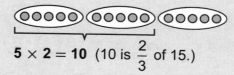

$5 \times 2 = 10$  (10 is $\frac{2}{3}$ of 15.)

**6.** Find the amounts using Keesha's method.

a) $\frac{3}{5}$ of 10 = _____

b) $\frac{1}{3}$ of 9 = _____

c) $\frac{2}{3}$ of 18 = _____

d) $\frac{2}{5}$ of 15 = _____

e) $\frac{2}{7}$ of 28 = _____

f) $\frac{3}{4}$ of 16 = _____

g) $\frac{1}{3}$ of 27 = _____

h) $\frac{1}{2}$ of 14 = _____

i) $\frac{3}{4}$ of 20 = _____

j) $\frac{4}{9}$ of 18 = _____

k) $\frac{5}{8}$ of 24 = _____

l) $\frac{2}{5}$ of 35 = _____

7.  a)  Shade $\frac{2}{5}$ of the squares.     b)  Shade $\frac{2}{3}$ of the squares.     c)  Shade $\frac{3}{4}$ of the squares.

    d)  Shade $\frac{5}{6}$ of the squares.

    e)  Shade $\frac{2}{7}$ of the squares.

8.  a)  Shade $\frac{1}{4}$ of the squares.

        Draw stripes in $\frac{1}{6}$ of the squares.

    b)  Shade $\frac{1}{3}$ of the squares.

        Draw stripes in $\frac{1}{6}$ of the squares.

        Put dots in $\frac{1}{8}$ of the squares.

9.  Each circle represents a child. Solve the problem by writing "J" for juice and "W" for water in the correct number of circles. The first one is done for you.

    a)  8 children had drinks at lunch.

        $\frac{1}{2}$ drank juice and $\frac{1}{4}$ drank water.

        Ⓙ Ⓙ Ⓦ ◯
        Ⓙ Ⓙ Ⓦ ◯

        How many didn't drink juice or water? _____2 didn't drink juice or water_____

    b)  6 children had drinks at lunch.

        $\frac{1}{2}$ drank juice and $\frac{1}{3}$ drank water.

        ◯ ◯ ◯
        ◯ ◯ ◯

        How many didn't drink juice or water? _____

10. 12 children had drinks. $\frac{1}{4}$ drank juice and $\frac{2}{3}$ drank water.

    How many didn't drink juice or water? Show your work.

11. There are 20 fish in an aquarium. $\frac{2}{5}$ are blue, $\frac{1}{4}$ are yellow, and the rest are green. How many are green?

12. Sofia has 18 books. $\frac{1}{9}$ are history, $\frac{2}{3}$ are fiction, and the rest are science books. How many science books does she have?

# 39. Multiplying Fractions by Whole Numbers

---

**REMINDER ▶** Multiplication is a short form for addition.

$$4 \times 5 = 5 + 5 + 5 + 5 \qquad 3 \times 6 = 6 + 6 + 6 \qquad 5 \times 8 = 8 + 8 + 8 + 8 + 8$$

---

**1.** Write the product as a sum.

a) $4 \times \dfrac{1}{5} = \dfrac{1}{5} + \dfrac{1}{5} + \dfrac{1}{5} + \dfrac{1}{5}$    b) $3 \times \dfrac{1}{4} =$    c) $5 \times \dfrac{2}{9} =$

**2.** Write the sum as a product.

a) $\dfrac{1}{4} + \dfrac{1}{4} + \dfrac{1}{4} =$    b) $\dfrac{4}{7} + \dfrac{4}{7} + \dfrac{4}{7} =$    c) $\dfrac{2}{3} + \dfrac{2}{3} + \dfrac{2}{3} + \dfrac{2}{3} + \dfrac{2}{3} =$

**3.** Find the product by first writing it as a sum.

a) $3 \times \dfrac{5}{7} = \dfrac{5}{7} + \dfrac{5}{7} + \dfrac{5}{7} = \dfrac{15}{7}$    b) $2 \times \dfrac{5}{9} =$

c) $4 \times \dfrac{6}{13} =$    d) $6 \times \dfrac{2}{5} =$

---

To multiply a fraction by a whole number, multiply the numerator by the whole number and leave the denominator the same. Example: $4 \times \dfrac{3}{5} = \dfrac{3}{5} + \dfrac{3}{5} + \dfrac{3}{5} + \dfrac{3}{5}$

$$= \dfrac{3 + 3 + 3 + 3}{5}$$

$$= \dfrac{12}{5} \longleftarrow 4 \times 3$$

---

**4.** Multiply the fraction by a whole number. Write your answer as a mixed number.

a) $2 \times \dfrac{5}{7} = \dfrac{10}{7} = 1\dfrac{3}{7}$    b) $4 \times \dfrac{2}{3} = \dfrac{\phantom{00}}{3} =$    c) $5 \times \dfrac{3}{8} = \dfrac{\phantom{00}}{8} =$

d) $6 \times \dfrac{3}{10} = \dfrac{\phantom{00}}{10} =$    e) $3 \times \dfrac{4}{5} = \dfrac{\phantom{00}}{5} =$    f) $7 \times \dfrac{5}{6} = \dfrac{\phantom{00}}{6} =$

**5.** Find the product. Simplify your answer. (Show your work in your notebook.)

a) $6 \times \dfrac{2}{3} = \dfrac{12}{3} = 4 \longleftarrow 12 \div 3$    b) $10 \times \dfrac{2}{5} =$    c) $4 \times \dfrac{3}{6} =$

d) $4 \times \dfrac{6}{8} =$    e) $6 \times \dfrac{3}{9} =$    f) $9 \times \dfrac{5}{9} =$

g) $8 \times \dfrac{3}{4} =$    h) $10 \times \dfrac{4}{8} =$    i) $12 \times \dfrac{5}{4} =$

---

In mathematics, the word "of" can mean multiply. Examples:

"2 groups of 3" means $2 \times 3 = 6$          "$\frac{1}{2}$ of 8" means $\frac{1}{2} \times 8 = 8 \div 2 = 4$

2 groups of 3          a group of 6          a group of 8

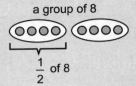

$\frac{1}{2}$ of 8

**6.** Calculate the product by calculating the fraction of the whole number.

a) $\frac{3}{4} \times 12 = \frac{3}{4}$ of $12 = $ __9__ ← $3 \times (12 \div 4)$          b) $\frac{2}{3} \times 6 = \frac{2}{3}$ of $6 = $ _____

c) $\frac{3}{5} \times 10 = $ _____          d) $\frac{1}{4} \times 20 = $ _____          e) $\frac{5}{6} \times 12 = $ _____          f) $\frac{3}{4} \times 16 = $ _____

---

Greg and Sam multiply the same numbers, $\frac{3}{5}$ and 10, but in a different order.

Greg: $\frac{3}{5} \times 10 = 3 \times (10 \div 5)$          Sam: $10 \times \frac{3}{5} = (10 \times 3) \div 5$

$\quad\quad\quad = 3 \times 2$          $\quad\quad\quad = 30 \div 5$

$\quad\quad\quad = 6$          $\quad\quad\quad = 6$

They get the same answer, 6.

---

**7.** a)  Multiply the same numbers, but in a different order.

i) $\frac{3}{4} \times 12$          and          $12 \times \frac{3}{4}$          ii) $\frac{2}{3} \times 6$          and          $6 \times \frac{2}{3}$

$= 3 \times (12 \div 4)$          $= (12 \times 3) \div 4$          $=$          $=$

$=$          $=$          $=$          $=$

$=$          $=$          $=$          $=$

iii) $\frac{1}{6} \times 12$ and $12 \times \frac{1}{6}$          iv) $\frac{2}{5} \times 15$ and $15 \times \frac{2}{5}$

b)  Do both products in each part of part a) have the same answer?
If not, find your mistake.

**8.** To make 1 pie, a recipe calls for $\frac{1}{4}$ of a cup of blueberries. How many cups of blueberries are needed for 8 pies?

**9.** Farah's exercise routine takes $\frac{1}{3}$ of an hour. She exercises 6 days a week. How many hours a week does she exercise?

# 40. Fractions Review

1. The pie chart shows the times of day when a lizard is active.

 awake but inactive

asleep

awake and active

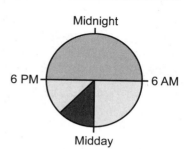

a) What fraction of the day is the lizard …

   i) awake but inactive?    ii) asleep?       iii) awake and active?

b) How many hours a day is the lizard …

   i) awake but inactive?    ii) asleep?       iii) awake and active?

2. Write four equivalent fractions for the amount shaded in the picture. Circle the fraction in lowest term.

 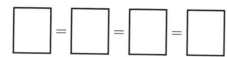

3. Steve's dog ate $\frac{2}{3}$ kg of dog food last month. This month, his dog ate $\frac{1}{4}$ kg less. How much dog food did Steve's dog eat this month?

4. Milena just turned 11 years old.

   How old was she $2\frac{1}{4}$ years ago?

5. Luis weighs $7\frac{1}{2}$ kg more than Ravi. If Ravi weighs $35\frac{1}{4}$ kg, how much does Luis weigh?

6. Mona ran $7\frac{3}{8}$ km in one hour, $5\frac{1}{4}$ km in the second hour, and $4\frac{1}{2}$ km in the third hour. How many kilometers did she run in three hours?

7. A salmon is $\frac{3}{5}$ yd long and a tuna is $\frac{4}{7}$ yd long.

   a) Which fish is longer? Explain how you know.

   b) How much longer is the longest fish?

# 41. Fractions and Division

Sarah wants to share a pie equally among four friends.

Each friend gets a quarter (or $\frac{1}{4}$ ) of the pie.

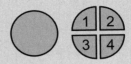

1. Shade how much one person gets. Write the fraction in the box.

   a) 2 people share a pancake equally.

   $\frac{1}{2}$

   b) 3 people share a gold bar equally.

   c) 5 people share a pentagon shape of chocolate equally.

   d) 8 people share a pizza equally.

2. Draw a picture to solve the problem.

   6 people share a pizza.

   How much pizza does each person get? _____

You can use the division sign (÷) for equal sharing, even when the answer is a fraction.

Example: When 3 people share a pancake equally, each person gets $\frac{1}{3}$ of a pancake. So $1 \div 3 = \frac{1}{3}$.

3. Write a unit fraction for the division statement.

   a) $1 \div 3 = \boxed{\frac{1}{3}}$   b) $1 \div 4 = \boxed{\phantom{x}}$   c) $1 \div 2 = \boxed{\phantom{x}}$   d) $1 \div 8 = \boxed{\phantom{x}}$

   e) $1 \div 10 = \boxed{\phantom{x}}$   f) $1 \div 20 = \boxed{\phantom{x}}$   g) $1 \div 25 = \boxed{\phantom{x}}$   h) $1 \div 100 = \boxed{\phantom{x}}$

4. Write a division statement for the unit fraction.

   a) $\frac{1}{6} = \underline{\ 1 \div 6\ }$   b) $\frac{1}{5} = \underline{\hspace{2cm}}$   c) $\frac{1}{12} = \underline{\hspace{2cm}}$   d) $\frac{1}{20} = \underline{\hspace{2cm}}$

   e) $\frac{1}{25} = \underline{\hspace{2cm}}$   f) $\frac{1}{8} = \underline{\hspace{2cm}}$   g) $\frac{1}{15} = \underline{\hspace{2cm}}$   h) $\frac{1}{50} = \underline{\hspace{2cm}}$

**Problem:** How can 4 people share 3 pies equally?

**Solution:** Share each pie equally.

One person takes the shaded pieces.

*There are 4 people, so cut each pie into 4 pieces.*

5. Determine the number of pieces and the number of whole pies.

   a)  3 people share 2 pies.

   Number of pieces in each pie: __3__

   Number of whole pies: __2__

   b)  2 people share 5 pies.

   Number of pieces in each pie: _____

   Number of whole pies: _____

   c)  3 people share 4 pies.

   Number of pieces in each pie: _____

   Number of whole pies: _____

   d)  5 people share 3 pies.

   Number of pieces in each pie: _____

   Number of whole pies: _____

6. Color one person's share of the pancakes. How much does each person get?

   a)  2 people share 3 pancakes.

   Each person gets $\dfrac{3}{2}$.

   b)  3 people share 2 pancakes.

   Each person gets ☐.

   c)  4 people share 2 pancakes.

   Each person gets ☐.

   d)  5 people share 3 pancakes.

   Each person gets ☐.

7. Draw a picture to solve the problem.

   3 people share 5 pizzas.

   How much pizza does each person get? _____

Four friends share 3 pies equally. Each friend gets 3 quarters of a pie, so $3 \div 4 = \dfrac{3}{4}$.

3 pies for 4 friends

$\dfrac{3}{4}$ for the first friend

$\dfrac{3}{4}$ for the second friend

$\dfrac{3}{4}$ for the third friend

$\dfrac{3}{4}$ for the fourth friend

**8.** Write a fraction for the division statement.

a) $2 \div 7 = \boxed{\dfrac{2}{7}}$

b) $4 \div 5 = \boxed{\phantom{x}}$

c) $3 \div 8 = \boxed{\phantom{x}}$

d) $5 \div 9 = \boxed{\phantom{x}}$

e) $5 \div 11 = \boxed{\phantom{x}}$

f) $9 \div 10 = \boxed{\phantom{x}}$

g) $10 \div 11 = \boxed{\phantom{x}}$

h) $15 \div 22 = \boxed{\phantom{x}}$

i) $23 \div 8 = \boxed{\phantom{x}}$

j) $32 \div 25 = \boxed{\phantom{x}}$

k) $43 \div 20 = \boxed{\phantom{x}}$

l) $173 \div 100 = \boxed{\phantom{x}}$

m) $19 \div 12 = \boxed{\phantom{x}}$

n) $88 \div 50 = \boxed{\phantom{x}}$

o) $56 \div 25 = \boxed{\phantom{x}}$

p) $67 \div 10 = \boxed{\phantom{x}}$

**9.** Write your answers to Question 8 parts i) to p) as mixed numbers.

a) $23 \div 8 = \boxed{2\dfrac{7}{8}}$

b) $32 \div 25 = \boxed{\phantom{x}}$

c) $43 \div 20 = \boxed{\phantom{x}}$

d) $173 \div 100 = \boxed{\phantom{x}}$

e) $19 \div 12 = \boxed{\phantom{x}}$

f) $88 \div 50 = \boxed{\phantom{x}}$

g) $56 \div 25 = \boxed{\phantom{x}}$

h) $67 \div 10 = \boxed{\phantom{x}}$

**10.** Write a division statement for the fraction. Then find the answer.

a) $\dfrac{6}{3} = \underline{\quad 6 \div 3 \quad} = \underline{\quad 2 \quad}$

b) $\dfrac{12}{4} = \underline{\hspace{3cm}} = \underline{\hspace{1.5cm}}$

c) $\dfrac{15}{3} = \underline{\hspace{3cm}} = \underline{\hspace{1.5cm}}$

d) $\dfrac{24}{6} = \underline{\hspace{3cm}} = \underline{\hspace{1.5cm}}$

e) $\dfrac{24}{4} = \underline{\hspace{3cm}} = \underline{\hspace{1.5cm}}$

f) $\dfrac{25}{5} = \underline{\hspace{3cm}} = \underline{\hspace{1.5cm}}$

g) $\dfrac{36}{9} = \underline{\hspace{3cm}} = \underline{\hspace{1.5cm}}$

h) $\dfrac{56}{8} = \underline{\hspace{3cm}} = \underline{\hspace{1.5cm}}$

**11.** Three friends want to share a 20-pound bag of rice equally by weight. How many pounds of rice should each friend get? Write your answer as a mixed number.

# 42. Multiplying Unit Fractions

1. Extend the horizontal lines to find out what fraction of the whole rectangle is shaded. Then write the fraction.

a)
$\dfrac{1}{6}$

b)
_____

c)
_____

d)
_____

---

Here is $\dfrac{1}{2}$ of a rectangle.

Here is $\dfrac{1}{3}$ of $\dfrac{1}{2}$ of the rectangle.

How much is $\dfrac{1}{3}$ of $\dfrac{1}{2}$?

Extend the lines to find out.

 $\dfrac{1}{3}$ of $\dfrac{1}{2} = \dfrac{1}{6}$

---

2. Extend the horizontal lines in the picture. Then complete a fraction statement for the picture using the word "of."

a)

$\dfrac{1}{3}$ of $\dfrac{1}{4} = \dfrac{1}{12}$

b)

$\dfrac{1}{3}$ of $\dfrac{1}{5} = $ ——

c)

$\dfrac{1}{2}$ of $\dfrac{1}{3} = $ ——

d)

$\dfrac{1}{4}$ of $\dfrac{1}{3} = $ ——

e)

$\dfrac{1}{5}$ of $\dfrac{1}{2} = $ ——

f)

$\dfrac{1}{4}$ of $\dfrac{1}{5} = $ ——

g)

$\dfrac{1}{5}$ of $\dfrac{1}{3} = $ ——

h)

$\dfrac{1}{4}$ of $\dfrac{1}{2} = $ ——

---

**REMINDER** ▶ The word "of" can mean "multiply."

Example: "$\dfrac{1}{2}$ of a group of 8" means $\dfrac{1}{2} \times 8 = 8 \div 2 = 4$.

---

3. Rewrite the fraction statements from Question 2 using the multiplication sign instead of the word "of."

a) $\dfrac{1}{3} \times \dfrac{1}{4} = \dfrac{1}{12}$     b)          c)          d)

e)          f)          g)          h)

**4.** Extend the horizontal lines. Then write a multiplication statement for the picture.

a)

$$\frac{1}{3} \times \frac{1}{2} = \frac{1}{6}$$

b)

c)

d)

e)

f)

g)

h)

Look at Question 4 a). How do you get the denominator of the answer from the other two denominators?

$$\frac{1}{3} \times \frac{1}{2} = \frac{1}{6} \longleftarrow 3 \times 2$$

**5.** Multiply.

a) $\frac{1}{2} \times \frac{1}{3} =$      b) $\frac{1}{4} \times \frac{1}{5} =$      c) $\frac{1}{5} \times \frac{1}{6} =$      d) $\frac{1}{7} \times \frac{1}{3} =$

e) $\frac{1}{3} \times \frac{1}{5} =$      f) $\frac{1}{5} \times \frac{1}{5} =$      g) $\frac{1}{5} \times \frac{1}{4} =$      h) $\frac{1}{5} \times \frac{1}{2} =$

i) $\frac{1}{4} \times \frac{1}{7} =$      j) $\frac{1}{6} \times \frac{1}{2} =$      k) $\frac{1}{3} \times \frac{1}{3} =$      l) $\frac{1}{7} \times \frac{1}{5} =$

**6.** Circle two multiplication statements in Question 5 that have the same answer.
How could you have predicted this?

**7.** Mike is making $\frac{1}{2}$ of a recipe for raisin bread.

The recipe calls for $\frac{1}{3}$ of a cup of raisins.

What fraction of a cup of raisins does Mike need?

**8.** There is $\frac{1}{3}$ of a pizza left. Clara eats $\frac{1}{4}$ of it.

What fraction of the whole pizza did Clara eat?

# 43. Multiplying Fractions

 Here is $\frac{2}{3}$ of a rectangle. |  Here is $\frac{4}{5}$ of $\frac{2}{3}$ of the rectangle. | How much is $\frac{4}{5}$ of $\frac{2}{3}$?

Extend the lines to find out.

 $\frac{4}{5}$ of $\frac{2}{3} = \frac{8}{15}$

1. Extend the horizontal lines in the picture. Then write a fraction statement for the picture using the word "of."

a)

$\frac{3}{4}$ of $\frac{2}{5} = \frac{6}{20}$

b)

—— of —— = ——

c)

—— of —— = ——

d)

—— of —— = ——

e)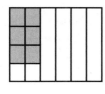

—— of —— = ——

f)

—— of —— = ——

g)

—— of —— = ——

h)

—— of —— = ——

---

$\frac{4}{5}$ of $\frac{2}{3} = \frac{8}{15}$ ← —— $4 \times 2$

—— $5 \times 3$

---

2. Rewrite the fraction statements from Question 1 using the multiplication sign instead of the word "of."

a) $\frac{3}{4} \times \frac{2}{5} = \frac{6}{20}$  b)  c)  d)

e)  f)  g)  h)

3. Multiply.

a) $\frac{2}{3} \times \frac{4}{7} = \frac{8}{21}$  b) $\frac{1}{2} \times \frac{3}{5} =$  c) $\frac{3}{4} \times \frac{5}{7} =$  d) $\frac{2}{3} \times \frac{10}{11} =$

e) $\frac{3}{4} \times \frac{3}{5} =$  f) $\frac{2}{5} \times \frac{4}{7} =$  BONUS ▶ $\frac{1}{2} \times \frac{3}{5} \times \frac{3}{7} =$

---

**4.** Ron is making $\frac{1}{2}$ of a recipe for pasta salad. The recipe calls for $\frac{3}{4}$ of a cup of bow tie pasta. What fraction of a cup of bow tie pasta does Ron need?

**5.** There is $\frac{3}{8}$ of a pie left. Grace eats $\frac{3}{5}$ of it. What fraction of the whole pie did Grace eat?

**6.** Sharira spends $\frac{3}{5}$ of her free time playing outside. She spends $\frac{2}{3}$ of her outside time playing soccer. What fraction of her free time did she play soccer?

You can multiply *improper fractions* the same way you multiply *proper fractions*.

$$\frac{5}{2} =$$

$$\frac{3}{4} \times \frac{5}{2} = \qquad = \frac{15}{8}$$ ⟵ 5 groups of 3 are shaded.
⟵ 2 groups of 4 are in each whole.

**7.** Multiply. Reduce your answer to lowest terms.

a) $\frac{2}{3} \times \frac{9}{4} = \frac{2 \times 9}{3 \times 4} = \frac{18}{12} = \frac{3}{2}$

b) $\frac{3}{4} \times \frac{12}{7} =$

c) $\frac{1}{2} \times \frac{8}{5} =$

d) $\frac{3}{2} \times \frac{6}{7} =$

e) $\frac{8}{3} \times \frac{7}{4} =$

f) $\frac{3}{5} \times \frac{15}{6} =$

g) $\frac{1}{6} \times \frac{12}{5} =$

**BONUS ▶** $\frac{11}{5} \times \frac{10}{33} =$

**8.** Ben believes $\frac{2}{3}$ of $\frac{8}{5}$ is greater than 1. Is he right? Explain.

**9.** Farah made apple juice. She used $\frac{3}{5}$ of a bag of apples on Saturday. She used $\frac{1}{2}$ of the rest of the apples on Sunday. What fraction of the bag did Farah use on Sunday? Reduce your answer to lowest terms.

# 44. Multiplying Mixed Numbers

1. Write the mixed number as an improper fraction.

a) $3\frac{1}{2} = \frac{7}{2}$ ← $3 \times 2 + 1$

b) $4\frac{1}{3} =$

c) $2\frac{3}{5} =$

d) $1\frac{4}{7} =$

---

Megan multiplies $3 \times 2\frac{1}{4}$ in three steps.

**Step 1**

Change the mixed number to an improper fraction.

Example:

$3 \times 2\frac{1}{4} = 3 \times \frac{9}{4}$ ← $2 \times 4 + 1$

**Step 2**

Multiply the improper fraction by the whole number.

$3 \times \frac{9}{4} = \frac{27}{4}$ ← $9 \times 3$

**Step 3**

Change the improper fraction to a mixed number.

$\frac{27}{4} = 6\frac{3}{4}$ ← $27 \div 4 = 6\,R\,3$

---

2. Change the mixed number to an improper fraction and multiply. Write your answer as a mixed number.

a) $2 \times 3\frac{2}{5} = 2 \times \frac{17}{5}$

$= \boxed{\dfrac{34}{5}}$ ← improper fraction

$= \boxed{6\frac{4}{5}}$ ← mixed number

b) $3 \times 4\frac{1}{2} =$

$= \Box$ ← improper fraction

$= \Box$ ← mixed number

c) $4 \times 1\frac{1}{3} =$

$= \Box$ ← improper fraction

$= \Box$ ← mixed number

d) $2\frac{3}{4} \times 6 =$

$= \Box$ ← improper fraction

$= \Box$ ← mixed number

e) $4\frac{2}{3} \times 2 =$

$= \Box$ ← improper fraction

$= \Box$ ← mixed number

f) $4 \times 1\frac{3}{5} =$

$= \Box$ ← improper fraction

$= \Box$ ← mixed number

g) $4 \times 2\frac{3}{10} =$

h) $3\frac{1}{5} \times 2 =$

i) $5\frac{1}{4} \times 3 =$

j) $2\frac{1}{6} \times 3 =$

Multiply two mixed numbers in three steps.

**Step 1**

Change the mixed numbers to improper fractions.

Example:

$$2\frac{3}{4} \times 1\frac{1}{2} = \frac{11}{4} \times \frac{3}{2}$$

(arrow: $2 \times 4 + 3$)

**Step 2**

Multiply the improper fractions.

$$\frac{11}{4} \times \frac{3}{2} = \frac{33}{8}$$

(arrow: $11 \times 3$)  (arrow: $4 \times 2$)

**Step 3**

Change the improper fraction to a mixed number.

$$\frac{33}{8} = 4\frac{1}{8}$$

(arrow: $33 \div 8 = 4 \text{ R } 1$)

---

3. Change the mixed numbers to improper fractions and multiply. Write your answer as a mixed number.

a) $1\frac{1}{3} \times 1\frac{3}{5} = \frac{4}{3} \times \frac{8}{5}$

$= \boxed{\dfrac{32}{15}}$ ← improper fraction

$= \boxed{2\dfrac{2}{15}}$ ← mixed number

b) $2\frac{3}{4} \times 3\frac{1}{2} =$

$= \boxed{\phantom{xx}}$ ← improper fraction

$= \boxed{\phantom{xx}}$ ← mixed number

c) $3\frac{1}{2} \times 2\frac{2}{3} =$

$= \boxed{\phantom{xx}}$ ← improper fraction

$= \boxed{\phantom{xx}}$ ← mixed number

d) $4\frac{2}{3} \times 2\frac{1}{5} =$

$= \boxed{\phantom{xx}}$ ← improper fraction

$= \boxed{\phantom{xx}}$ ← mixed number

e) $3\frac{1}{3} \times 2\frac{7}{10} =$

f) $1\frac{2}{3} \times 2\frac{1}{5} =$

g) $2\frac{1}{4} \times 1\frac{2}{5} =$

h) $2\frac{1}{3} \times 2\frac{2}{5} =$

4. Luis is making $\frac{3}{5}$ of a recipe for mushroom soup. The recipe calls for $3\frac{1}{2}$ cups of milk

a) How much milk does he need? Hint: Change $3\frac{1}{2}$ to an improper fraction.

b) Luis uses 2 cups of milk. Will his recipe work?

5. Nina is making $3\frac{1}{2}$ batches of cookies. The recipe for one batch calls for $1\frac{3}{4}$ cups of flour.

a) How many cups of flour does Nina need?

b) She has 6 cups of flour. If she uses all her flour, will the recipe work?

---

# 45. Multiplication and Fractions

1. Find the product. The fractions in the questions are all *smaller than 1*. Compare your answer to the whole number.

   a) $\dfrac{2}{3} \times 6 = \dfrac{12}{3} = 4$

   $\dfrac{2}{3} \times 6$ is ___smaller___ than 6.

   b) $\dfrac{3}{4} \times 8 = \dfrac{\phantom{00}}{4} =$

   $\dfrac{3}{4} \times 8$ is _____ than 8.

   c) $\dfrac{2}{5} \times 10 = \dfrac{\phantom{00}}{5} =$

   $\dfrac{2}{5} \times 10$ is _____ than 10.

   d) $\dfrac{5}{6} \times 12 = \dfrac{\phantom{00}}{6} =$

   $\dfrac{5}{6} \times 12$ is _____ than 12.

   e) $\dfrac{4}{8} \times 6 = \dfrac{\phantom{00}}{8} =$

   $\dfrac{4}{8} \times 6$ is _____ than 6.

   f) $\dfrac{3}{12} \times 8 = \dfrac{\phantom{00}}{12} =$

   $\dfrac{3}{12} \times 8$ is _____ than 8.

2. When you multiply a whole number by a fraction smaller than 1, do you think the answer will be less than the whole number or greater than the whole number?

   _____

---

To find $\dfrac{2}{3} \times 9$ or $\dfrac{2}{3}$ of 9 ...

**Step 1:** Divide 9 into 3 equal parts.

**Step 2:** Select 2 of the parts.

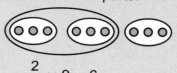

$\dfrac{2}{3} \times 9 = 6$

---

3. Draw a picture to find the product.

   a) $\dfrac{3}{4} \times 12$ or $\dfrac{3}{4}$ of 12

   b) $\dfrac{2}{3} \times 6$ or $\dfrac{2}{3}$ of 6

   c) $\dfrac{3}{4} \times 8$ or $\dfrac{3}{4}$ of 8

   d) $\dfrac{4}{5} \times 15$ or $\dfrac{4}{5}$ of 15

   e) $\dfrac{5}{6} \times 12$ or $\dfrac{5}{6}$ of 12

4. State the meaning of the product.

   a) $\dfrac{3}{5} \times 15$

   Divide __15__ into __5__ parts.

   Select __3__ of the parts.

   b) $\dfrac{2}{3} \times 12$

   Divide _____ into _____ parts.

   Select _____ of the parts.

   c) $\dfrac{2}{5} \times 10$

   Divide _____ into _____ parts.

   Select _____ of the parts.

**5.** Draw a picture to show why $\frac{4}{5}$ of 20 is less than 20.

**6.** Find the product. The fractions in the questions are all *greater than 1*. Compare your answer to the whole number.

a) $\frac{5}{4} \times 8 = \frac{40}{4} = 10$

   $\frac{5}{4} \times 8$ is ___*larger*___ than 8.

b) $\frac{4}{3} \times 6 = \frac{\phantom{00}}{3} =$

   $\frac{4}{3} \times 6$ is _____ than 6.

c) $\frac{6}{5} \times 10 = \frac{\phantom{00}}{5} =$

   $\frac{6}{5} \times 10$ is _____ than 10.

d) $\frac{8}{6} \times 12 = \frac{\phantom{00}}{6} =$

   $\frac{8}{6} \times 12$ is _____ than 12.

e) $\frac{5}{2} \times 6 = \frac{\phantom{00}}{2} =$

   $\frac{5}{2} \times 6$ is _____ than 6.

f) $\frac{10}{9} \times 18 = \frac{\phantom{00}}{9} =$

   $\frac{10}{9} \times 18$ is _____ than 18.

**7.** When you multiply a whole number by a fraction greater than 1, do you think the answer will be less than the whole number or greater than the whole number?

_____

**8.** Rewrite the product in expanded form.

a) $1\frac{1}{2} \times 3 = \left(1 + \frac{1}{2}\right) \times 3$

   $= 1 \times 3 + \frac{1}{2} \times 3$

b) $1\frac{3}{4} \times 5 = \left(\underline{\phantom{0}} + \underline{\phantom{0}}\right) \times \underline{\phantom{0}}$

   $= \underline{\phantom{000}} + \underline{\phantom{000}}$

c) $1\frac{5}{6} \times 2 = \left(\underline{\phantom{0}} + \underline{\phantom{0}}\right) \times \underline{\phantom{0}}$

   $= \underline{\phantom{000}} + \underline{\phantom{000}}$

**9.** Explain why $1\frac{1}{2} \times 3$ must be greater than 3. Hint: Use your work from Question 8.

**10.** Explain why $\frac{5}{4} \times 7$ must be greater than 7. Hint: Change $\frac{5}{4}$ to a mixed number.

**11.** Predict whether the product will be greater than or less than $\frac{1}{2}$. Then find the product.

a) $\frac{2}{3} \times \frac{1}{2}$ is _____ than $\frac{1}{2}$

   $\frac{2}{3} \times \frac{1}{2} = \boxed{\phantom{00}}$

b) $\frac{6}{5} \times \frac{1}{2}$ is _____ than $\frac{1}{2}$

   $\frac{6}{5} \times \frac{1}{2} = \boxed{\phantom{00}}$

**12.** Alex has 12 stickers. Maria has $1\frac{1}{4}$ times as many as Alex. Sofia has $\frac{5}{6}$ as many as Alex.

a) Without calculating, say who has the greatest number of stickers. Explain your answer.

b) To check your answer in part a), calculate the number of stickers for Maria and Sofia.

---

# 46. Scaling

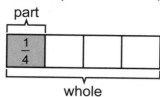

part = whole × $\dfrac{1}{4}$ ⟵ Scale factor is $\dfrac{1}{4}$.

whole = part × 4 ⟵ Scale factor is 4.

1. Using a ruler and the scale factor given, extend the drawing to show the whole.

a)
$\dfrac{1}{2}$

Scale factor = 2

b)
$\dfrac{1}{3}$

Scale factor = 3

c)
$\dfrac{1}{4}$

Scale factor = 4

d)
$\dfrac{1}{5}$

Scale factor = 5

2. Using a ruler and the scale factor given, shade to show the part.

a)

Scale factor = $\dfrac{1}{2}$

b)

Scale factor = $\dfrac{1}{3}$

3. Using a ruler, find what fraction of the box is shaded. What is the scale factor?

a)

$\dfrac{1}{3}$ is shaded

whole = part × __3__

part = whole × $\boxed{\dfrac{1}{3}}$

b)

—— is shaded

whole = part × _____

part = whole × $\boxed{\phantom{x}}$

c)

—— is shaded

whole = part × _____

part = whole × $\boxed{\phantom{x}}$

d)

—— is shaded

whole = part × _____

part = whole × $\boxed{\phantom{x}}$

**4.** For the bold number, circle the number that is $\frac{1}{2}$ and draw a box around the number that is double.

a)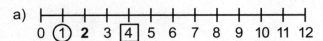

b)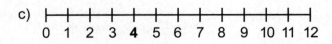

c)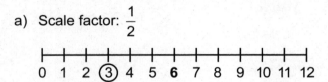

**BONUS ▶**

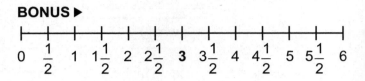

**5.** Multiply 6 by the scale factor. Circle the answer on the number line.

a) Scale factor: $\frac{1}{2}$

b) Scale factor: $\frac{1}{3}$

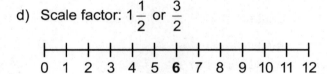

c) Scale factor: 2

d) Scale factor: $1\frac{1}{2}$ or $\frac{3}{2}$

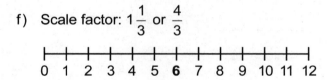

e) Scale factor: $\frac{2}{3}$

f) Scale factor: $1\frac{1}{3}$ or $\frac{4}{3}$

---

**REMINDER ▶** Multiplying by a scale factor smaller than 1 makes the number smaller.

Multiplying by a scale factor larger than 1 makes the number larger.

---

**6.** Multiply the number by the scale factor.

a) 5 by the scale factor $\frac{1}{2}$

$$5 \times \frac{1}{2} = \frac{5}{2} = 2\frac{1}{2}$$

b) 7 by the scale factor $\frac{1}{3}$

c) $\frac{1}{2}$ by the scale factor 3

d) 3 by the scale factor 2

 **BONUS ▶** On a map, 1 cm represents 500 m.

a) If a lake is 6 cm long on the map, what is the actual size of the lake?

b) The distance between the forest and the ocean in real life is 1,000 m. What is the distance on the map?

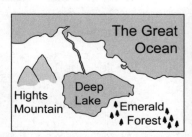

# 47. Word Problems with Fractions and Multiplication

**1.** A foot is 12 inches. A yard is 3 feet. What fraction of a yard is 8 inches?

Find what fraction of a foot 8 inches is: *8 inches is $\frac{8}{12}$ of a foot.*

Find what fraction of a yard a foot is: *1 foot is $\frac{1}{3}$ of a yard.*

So 8 inches $= \frac{8}{12} \times \frac{1}{3}$ of a yard $=$ _____ of a yard.

---

**2.** A year has _____ months.

A decade has _____ years.

What fraction of a decade is 8 months? _____

**3.** A century has 100 years. A year has 52 weeks.

What fraction of a century is 13 weeks? _____

---

**4.** A day has 24 hours. An hour has 60 minutes.

What fraction of a day is 45 minutes?

**BONUS ▶** What fraction of a day is 40 seconds?

**5.** How many months old is a $1\frac{2}{3}$-year-old child?

---

**6.** a) Anwar has $\frac{7}{5}$ cups of flour. He uses $\frac{3}{4}$ of it to bake a cake. How much flour did he use?

b) Did Anwar use more or less than 1 cup of flour? How do you know?

**7.** Kim has $\frac{5}{3}$ cups of paint. She uses $\frac{3}{4}$ of it to paint a shelf.

a) How much paint did she use?

b) Did Kim use more or less than 1 cup of paint? How do you know?

---

**8.** Leo has $\frac{11}{5}$ teaspoons of salt. He uses $\frac{1}{3}$ of it to cook a pot of soup. He then eats $\frac{2}{9}$ of the soup. How much salt did Leo eat?

**BONUS ▶** The peel of a banana weighs $\frac{1}{8}$ of the total weight of a banana. You buy 6 kg of bananas at $0.50 per kg. How much do you pay for the peel?

---

# 48. Dividing Fractions by Whole Numbers

1. One half of the whole rectangle is shaded. What fraction of the whole rectangle is striped? Hint: How many striped pieces fit into the whole rectangle?

a)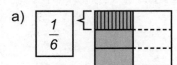

b)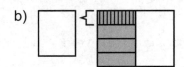

c)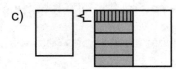

2. What is the area of the striped part? Hint: Extend the lines to divide the rectangle into smaller parts.

a) $\dfrac{1}{12}$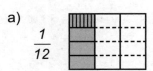

b) ___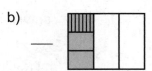

c) ___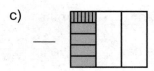

d) ___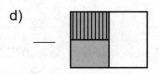

e) ___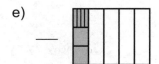

f) ___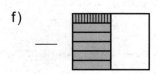

g) ___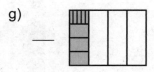

h) ___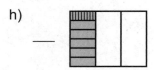

i) ___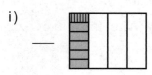

j) ___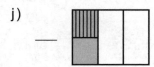

k) ___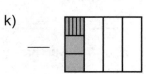

l) ___

The model in Question 2.a) shows that $\dfrac{1}{3} \div 4 = \dfrac{1}{12}$ because $\dfrac{1}{3}$ of the whole rectangle is divided into 4 smaller parts.

3. Write a division statement for each model in Question 2.

a) $\dfrac{1}{3} \div 4 = \dfrac{1}{12}$

b)

c)

d)

e)

f)

g)

h)

i)

j)

k)

l)

Five people share $\frac{2}{3}$ of a cake. What fraction of the cake does each person get?

Divide $\frac{2}{3}$ into 5 equal groups. How much is in each group?

 so $\frac{2}{3} \div 5 = \frac{2}{15}$

**4.** Use the model to divide each fraction.

a)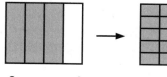

$\frac{3}{4} \div 5 = \frac{3}{20}$

b)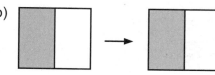

$\frac{1}{2} \div 3 =$

c)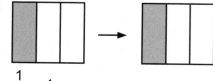

$\frac{1}{3} \div 4 =$

d)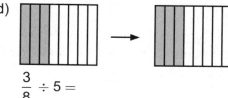

$\frac{3}{8} \div 5 =$

**5.** Finish the model to divide.

a)

$\frac{1}{2} \div 3 = \frac{1}{6}$

b)

$\frac{2}{3} \div 5 =$

c)

$\frac{1}{3} \div 4 =$

d)

$\frac{3}{5} \div 4 =$

**6.** Check your answers to Question 5 using multiplication. Example: Does $3 \times \frac{1}{6} = \frac{1}{2}$?

$$\frac{2}{5} \div 3 = \frac{2}{5 \times 3} = \frac{2}{15}$$

**7.** Divide. Check your answers using a model.

a) $\frac{3}{5} \div 2 =$  b) $\frac{1}{7} \div 4 =$  c) $\frac{4}{5} \div 3 =$  d) $\frac{2}{3} \div 3 =$

**8.** Five people share $\frac{5}{8}$ of a cake equally. What fraction of the cake does each person eat?

**9.** Four people share $\frac{1}{2}$ lb of almonds equally. How much does each person get?

You can divide improper fractions by whole numbers the same way you divide proper fractions.

$$\frac{5}{2} =$$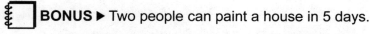

$$\frac{5}{2} \div 4 = \qquad = \frac{5}{8} \longleftarrow \quad 2 \times 4$$

**10.** Divide.

a) $\dfrac{5}{4} \div 2 = \dfrac{5}{4 \times 2} = \dfrac{5}{8}$

b) $\dfrac{5}{2} \div 3 = \underline{\qquad} = \underline{\quad}$

c) $\dfrac{7}{4} \div 5 = \underline{\qquad} = \underline{\quad}$

d) $\dfrac{8}{3} \div 6 = \underline{\qquad} = \underline{\quad}$

Divide mixed numbers by whole numbers in three steps.

**Step 1**

Change the mixed number to an improper fraction.

Example: $\overset{5 \times 4 + 3}{\nearrow}$

$5\dfrac{3}{4} \div 2 = \dfrac{23}{4} \div 2$

**Step 2**

Divide the improper fraction.

$\dfrac{23}{4} \div 2 = \dfrac{23}{4 \times 2} = \dfrac{23}{8}$

**Step 3**

Change the improper fraction to a mixed number.

$\overset{23 \div 8 = 2\,R\,7}{\nearrow}$

$\dfrac{23}{8} = 2\dfrac{7}{8}$

**11.** Divide by changing the mixed number to an improper fraction.

a) $2\dfrac{3}{4} \div 5 = \dfrac{11}{4} \div 5 = \dfrac{11}{4 \times 5} = \dfrac{11}{20}$

b) $2\dfrac{1}{2} \div 3 = \dfrac{\quad}{\quad} \div 3 = \underline{\qquad} = \underline{\quad}$

c) $1\dfrac{3}{4} \div 5 = \dfrac{\quad}{\quad} \div 5 = \underline{\qquad} = \underline{\quad}$

d) $2\dfrac{2}{3} \div 6 = \dfrac{\quad}{\quad} \div 6 = \underline{\qquad} = \underline{\quad}$

e) $3\dfrac{2}{5} \div 4 = \dfrac{\quad}{\quad} \div 4 = \underline{\qquad} = \underline{\quad}$

f) $1\dfrac{4}{7} \div 2 = \dfrac{\quad}{\quad} \div 2 = \underline{\qquad} = \underline{\quad}$

**12.** Three people share $1\dfrac{1}{2}$ pizzas equally. What fraction of the pizzas does each person eat?

**BONUS ▶** Two people can paint a house in 5 days.

a) How long does it take 5 people to paint that house?

b) How long does it take 4 people to paint that house?

# 49. Dividing Whole Numbers by Unit Fractions

There are 4 quarters in one whole.

So $1 \div \dfrac{1}{4} = 4$.

| | 1 | | |
|---|---|---|---|
| $\frac{1}{4}$ | $\frac{1}{4}$ | $\frac{1}{4}$ | $\frac{1}{4}$ |

1. How many fit into 1?

a)

| 1 | |
|---|---|
| $\frac{1}{2}$ | $\frac{1}{2}$ |

The number of $\dfrac{1}{2}$s in a whole is ___2___.

b)

| | 1 | | | |
|---|---|---|---|---|
| $\frac{1}{5}$ | $\frac{1}{5}$ | $\frac{1}{5}$ | $\frac{1}{5}$ | $\frac{1}{5}$ |

The number of $\dfrac{1}{5}$s in a whole is _____.

c)

| | 1 | |
|---|---|---|
| $\frac{1}{3}$ | $\frac{1}{3}$ | $\frac{1}{3}$ |

The number of $\dfrac{1}{3}$s in a whole is _____.

d)

| | | 1 | | | |
|---|---|---|---|---|---|
| $\frac{1}{6}$ | $\frac{1}{6}$ | $\frac{1}{6}$ | $\frac{1}{6}$ | $\frac{1}{6}$ | $\frac{1}{6}$ |

The number of $\dfrac{1}{6}$s in a whole is _____.

2. Complete the division statement using your answers from Question 1.

a) $1 \div \dfrac{1}{2} =$ ___2___      b) $1 \div \dfrac{1}{5} =$ _____      c) $1 \div \dfrac{1}{3} =$ _____      d) $1 \div \dfrac{1}{6} =$ _____

There are 4 quarters in each whole, so there are 8 quarters in two wholes.

So $2 \div \dfrac{1}{4} = 8$.

| | 1 | | | | 1 | | |
|---|---|---|---|---|---|---|---|
| $\frac{1}{4}$ | $\frac{1}{4}$ | $\frac{1}{4}$ | $\frac{1}{4}$ | $\frac{1}{4}$ | $\frac{1}{4}$ | $\frac{1}{4}$ | $\frac{1}{4}$ |

3. How many fit into 2?

a)

| 1 | | 1 | |
|---|---|---|---|
| $\frac{1}{2}$ | $\frac{1}{2}$ | $\frac{1}{2}$ | $\frac{1}{2}$ |

$2 \div \dfrac{1}{2} =$ _____

b)

| | 1 | | | 1 | |
|---|---|---|---|---|---|
| $\frac{1}{3}$ | $\frac{1}{3}$ | $\frac{1}{3}$ | $\frac{1}{3}$ | $\frac{1}{3}$ | $\frac{1}{3}$ |

$2 \div \dfrac{1}{3} =$ _____

c) $2 \div \dfrac{1}{5} =$ _____

d) $2 \div \dfrac{1}{10} =$ _____

**4.** Write a division statement for the picture.

a)

| 1 | | 1 | | 1 | |
|---|---|---|---|---|---|
| $\frac{1}{2}$ | $\frac{1}{2}$ | $\frac{1}{2}$ | $\frac{1}{2}$ | $\frac{1}{2}$ | $\frac{1}{2}$ |

$3 \div \frac{1}{2} = 6$

b)

| 1 | | | | 1 | | | |
|---|---|---|---|---|---|---|---|
| $\frac{1}{4}$ | $\frac{1}{4}$ | $\frac{1}{4}$ | $\frac{1}{4}$ | $\frac{1}{4}$ | $\frac{1}{4}$ | $\frac{1}{4}$ | $\frac{1}{4}$ |

_____

c)

| 1 | | | | | 1 | | | | | 1 | | | | |
|---|---|---|---|---|---|---|---|---|---|---|---|---|---|---|
| $\frac{1}{5}$ | $\frac{1}{5}$ | $\frac{1}{5}$ | $\frac{1}{5}$ | $\frac{1}{5}$ | $\frac{1}{5}$ | $\frac{1}{5}$ | $\frac{1}{5}$ | $\frac{1}{5}$ | $\frac{1}{5}$ | $\frac{1}{5}$ | $\frac{1}{5}$ | $\frac{1}{5}$ | $\frac{1}{5}$ | $\frac{1}{5}$ |

_____

**5.** Use the number line to decide how many steps of size $\frac{1}{3}$ fit into 4.

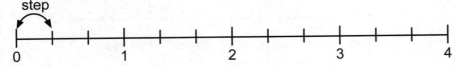

Write the division statement. _____

**6.** Draw a number line to divide 4 by $\frac{1}{2}$. Then write the division statement.

---

How many $\frac{1}{3}$s fit into 5? Three $\frac{1}{3}$s fit into 1, so 5 times as many fit into 5.　　$5 \div \frac{1}{3} = 5 \times 3 = 15$

---

**7.** Divide.

a) $2 \div \frac{1}{3} = \underline{\ \ 2\ \ } \times \underline{\ \ 3\ \ } = \underline{\ \ 6\ \ }$

b) $4 \div \frac{1}{3} = \underline{\ \ \ \ } \times \underline{\ \ \ \ \ } = \underline{\ \ \ \ \ }$

c) $3 \div \frac{1}{2} = \underline{\ \ \ \ } \times \underline{\ \ \ \ \ } = \underline{\ \ \ \ \ }$

d) $5 \div \frac{1}{2} = \underline{\ \ \ \ } \times \underline{\ \ \ \ \ } = \underline{\ \ \ \ \ }$

e) $6 \div \frac{1}{4} = \underline{\ \ \ \ } \times \underline{\ \ \ \ \ } = \underline{\ \ \ \ \ }$

f) $4 \div \frac{1}{6} = \underline{\ \ \ \ } \times \underline{\ \ \ \ \ } = \underline{\ \ \ \ \ }$

**8.** a) Ethan has a scoop that measures a $\frac{1}{2}$ cup. He needs 3 cups of flour. How many scoopfuls of flour does he need?

b) Alice has 2 chocolate bars. She cuts each chocolate bar into quarters. How many pieces does she have?

# 50. Word Problems with Fractions and Division

**1.** Greg jogs $\frac{1}{2}$ km in 3 minutes. How far does he jog in 1 minute?

$\frac{1}{2} \div 3 =$ _____ km

---

**2.** a) A cake recipe uses $\frac{3}{4}$ cups of sugar.
   The cake is divided into 6 pieces.
   How much sugar is in each piece?

   b) Another cake recipe uses $1\frac{1}{3}$ cups of sugar.
   The cake is divided into 8 pieces.
   How much sugar is in each piece?

**3.** Rosa invites friends for dinner. She has $\frac{6}{8}$ kg of dry spaghetti. Each person needs $\frac{3}{16}$ kg. How many people can she feed?

---

**4.** A rope is $4\frac{4}{5}$ m long. It is divided equally into 12 pieces. How long is each piece?

**5.** If 5 egg cartons weigh $3\frac{1}{2}$ pounds, find the weight of one carton.

---

**6.** a) What fraction of a year is a month?
   b) What fraction of a decade is a year?
   c) What fraction of a decade is a month?

**7.** A bookshelf is 26 inches wide. How many $\frac{1}{2}$-inch wide books can fit on the bookshelf?

---

**BONUS ▶** A string is $3\frac{1}{2}$ m long. It is divided into 5 equal parts. How long is each piece?

$3\frac{1}{2} \div 5 = \frac{7}{2} \div 5 =$ _____ m = _____ cm

---

# 51. Word Problems with Fractions, Multiplication, and Division

**1.** Craig has $48 dollars. He spends $\frac{1}{4}$ of his money on a book and $\frac{3}{8}$ on a pair of gloves.

   a) How many dollars did Craig spend on the gloves?

   b) How much money does he have left?

**2.** Ben and Kevin mow the grass in a backyard. Ben mows $\frac{3}{5}$ of the yard and Kevin mows the rest.

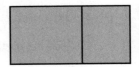

   a) What fraction of the yard did Kevin mow?

   b) The yard is 30 m long. How long is each person's section?

**3.** Sally stretches for $\frac{1}{2}$ an hour, walks for $\frac{2}{3}$ of an hour, and jogs for $\frac{2}{5}$ of an hour.

Use two methods to calculate how many minutes she exercised.

   a) Add the fractions and then convert to minutes.

   b) Convert the fractions to minutes and then add.

   c) Did you get the same answers from parts a) and b)?

**4.** Ivan talks on the phone for $\frac{1}{5}$ of an hour. Jake talks on the phone for $\frac{1}{100}$ of a day.

Who talked longer on the phone?

**5.** Sofia does one jumping jack in 2 seconds. How many jumping jacks can she do in $\frac{7}{10}$ of a minute? Circle the correct formula.

$$\frac{7}{10} \times 2 \qquad \frac{7}{10} \div 2 \qquad 2 \div \frac{7}{10} \qquad 42 \div 2 \qquad 2 \div 42$$

Explain your choice. _____

_____

---

Use the information in this box to answer Questions 6 to 9.

Jade spends $\frac{3}{4}$ of an hour doing math homework, $\frac{2}{5}$ of an hour doing geography, and $\frac{5}{6}$ of an hour doing science.

---

**6.** Compare fractions to answer the questions.

   a) Did Jade spend more or less than half an hour doing geography?

   b) Did Jade spend more time doing math or science?

7. Decide whether the problem requires addition, subtraction, multiplication, or division. Then solve the problem.

a) Jade spends $\frac{1}{3}$ of her time doing math homework working on word problems. What fraction of an hour did she spend on word problems?

b) How many hours did Jade spend on homework altogether?

c) How many more hours did Jade spend on science than on geography?

d) Jade divides her time on geography evenly between reading the textbook and answering questions. What fraction of an hour did she spend reading the textbook?

8. Solve the problems.

a) Jade has 2 hours to do her homework before she has to leave to meet a friend.

How many minutes before she has to leave did Jade finish her homework?

b) Jade spends $\frac{1}{3}$ of her time on science reading the textbook. She spends $\frac{1}{5}$

of her remaining time on science doing calculations. How many hours did she spend on calculations?

9. a) Jade's sister spends $\frac{1}{3}$ the amount of time Jade does on math, but twice the

amount of time on geography and $1\frac{1}{2}$ times as much time on science.

Who spent more time doing homework, Jade or her sister?

b) Jade's brother spends the same total amount of time on homework as Jade's sister. He spends the same amount of time on all three subjects. How much time did Jade's brother spend on each subject? Write your answer as a fraction of an hour.

c) Jade's sister spends $\frac{1}{5}$ of her time on science reading the textbook.

Who spent more time reading her science textbook, Jade or her sister?

10. Make up a word problem that requires finding:

a) $\frac{4}{5} + \frac{1}{3}$      b) $\frac{4}{5} - \frac{1}{3}$      c) $\frac{4}{5} \times \frac{1}{3}$      d) $\frac{4}{5} \div \frac{1}{3}$

# 52. Comparing Fractions Using Benchmarks

1. Name the shaded fraction.

a)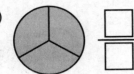

b)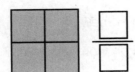

c)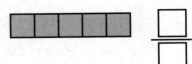

2. A fraction is equivalent to 1 if its numerator and denominator are _____.

3. Circle the fraction equivalent to 1. Then write if the fractions are "more" or "less" than 1.

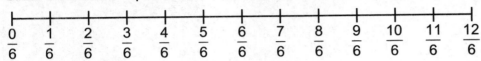

a) $\frac{5}{6}$ is _____ than 1.

b) $\frac{11}{6}$ is _____ than 1.

> A fraction is less than 1 if the numerator is less than the denominator. Example: $\frac{2}{3}$ is less than 1.
>
> A fraction is greater than 1 if the numerator is greater than the denominator. Example: $\frac{5}{4}$ is greater than 1.

4. Is the fraction less than or greater than 1? Write > (greater than) or < (less than).

a) $\frac{7}{8}$ ☐ 1

b) $\frac{4}{7}$ ☐ 1

c) $\frac{14}{13}$ ☐ 1

d) $\frac{23}{24}$ ☐ 1

5. Circle the fraction equivalent to $\frac{1}{2}$ on the number line.

a)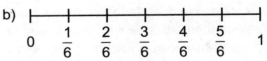

b)

> A fraction is equal to half if double the numerator is equal to the denominator.
>
> Example: $\frac{5}{10}$ is equal to $\frac{1}{2}$ because the double of 5 is equal to 10.

6. Fill in the blank.

a) $\frac{1}{2} = \frac{7}{14}$

b) $\frac{1}{2} = \frac{30}{\quad}$

c) $\frac{1}{2} = \frac{\quad}{800}$

d) $\frac{1}{2} = \frac{43}{\quad}$

A fraction is less than half if double the numerator is less than the denominator.

Example: $\frac{4}{9}$ is less than $\frac{1}{2}$ because the double of 4 is less than 9.

A fraction is more than half if double the numerator is more than the denominator.

Example: $\frac{3}{5}$ is more than $\frac{1}{2}$ because the double of 3 is more than 5.

7.  Write > (greater than), < (less than), or = (equal to).

a) $\frac{3}{8}$ ☐ $\frac{1}{2}$

b) $\frac{4}{7}$ ☐ $\frac{1}{2}$

c) $\frac{13}{25}$ ☐ $\frac{1}{2}$

d) $\frac{1}{2}$ ☐ $\frac{23}{50}$

e) $\frac{18}{36}$ ☐ $\frac{1}{2}$

f) $\frac{9}{17}$ ☐ $\frac{1}{2}$

g) $\frac{1}{2}$ ☐ $\frac{14}{29}$

h) $\frac{37}{72}$ ☐ $\frac{1}{2}$

8.  Write "greater" or "less."

a) $\frac{1}{4}$ is _____ than $\frac{1}{2}$ and $\frac{1}{2}$ is _____ than $\frac{4}{6}$, so $\frac{1}{4}$ is _____ than $\frac{4}{6}$.

b) $\frac{53}{100}$ is _____ than $\frac{1}{2}$ and $\frac{1}{2}$ is _____ than $\frac{3}{7}$, so $\frac{53}{100}$ is _____ than $\frac{3}{7}$.

9.  Karen eats $\frac{3}{8}$ of a pizza. Is that more or less than half the pizza? _____

10. In a Grade 5 class, $\frac{4}{9}$ of the students are girls. Are there more girls or boys in the class? Explain.

11. On a baseball team, $\frac{6}{11}$ of the players are girls.

Are there more girls or boys on the team?

12. Ron eats $\frac{3}{5}$ of a pizza, and Karen eats $\frac{1}{3}$ of the pizza.

Who ate more pizza? Explain how you know.

13. Maria thinks that $\frac{4}{3}$ is less than $\frac{99}{100}$ because the numbers are smaller. Is she right?

Explain how you know.

14. Is $\frac{3}{10}$ of $\frac{4}{3}$ less than or greater than $\frac{1}{2}$? Explain.

# 53. Cumulative Review

1. $\frac{2}{100}$ of Antarctica is *not* covered in ice.
   What fraction of Antarctica is covered in ice?

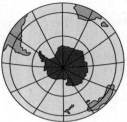

2. Mia runs around a field 6 times in a $\frac{1}{2}$ hour.

   The distance around the field is 0.5 miles.

   How far can she run in an hour?

3. Seven classes at Washington Elementary School are going skiing.

   There are 22 students in each class.

   The teachers order 6 buses, which each hold 26 students. Will there be enough room? Explain.

4. It takes Kim 40 minutes to finish her homework: she spends $\frac{2}{5}$ of the time on math and $\frac{2}{5}$ of the time on science.

   a) How many minutes did she spend on math and science?

   b) How many minutes did she spend on other subjects?

   c) What fraction of the time did she spend on other subjects?

5. Eric bikes $11\frac{7}{8}$ miles on Saturday.

   He bikes $3\frac{1}{4}$ fewer miles on Sunday.

   a) About how many miles did Eric bike on Sunday?

   b) About how many miles did he bike in total?

6. Ron buys $\frac{8}{3}$ cups of sugar. He uses $\frac{1}{4}$ of it to bake muffins. He then eats $\frac{1}{6}$ of the muffins.

   How much sugar did he eat?

7. A ball is dropped from a height of 24 m. Each time it hits the ground, it bounces $\frac{3}{4}$ of the last height. How high did it bounce …

   a) on the first bounce?

   b) on the second bounce?

8. John earns $16.54 on Monday and adds it to his savings.

   On Friday, he spends half of his money on a T-shirt. He now has $14.37.

   How much money did he have before he started work Monday?

110

JUMP Math Accumula

9. A pentagonal box has a perimeter of $3\frac{3}{4}$ m. How long is each side?

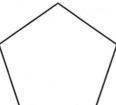

10. Roberto, Kendra, and Nathan paint a whole wall. Roberto paints $\frac{2}{5}$ of the wall and Kendra paints $\frac{1}{3}$.

| Roberto | Kendra | Nathan |
|---|---|---|
| $\frac{2}{5}$ | $\frac{1}{3}$ | ? |

← —— 30 m —— →

a) What fraction of the wall did Nathan paint?

b) Each person paints a rectangular section. The wall is 30 m long. How long is each person's section?

11. Find the mystery numbers.

a) I am a number between 25 and 35. I am a multiple of 3 and 5.

b) I am a number between 10 and 20. My tens digit is 1 less than my ones digit.

c) Rounded to the nearest tens, I am 40. I am an even number. The difference in my digits is 3.

12. Tom gives away $\frac{3}{4}$ of his hockey cards.

a) What fraction of his cards did he keep?

b) Tom puts his remaining cards in a scrapbook. Each page holds 14 cards. He fills 23 pages. How many cards did he put in the book?

c) How many cards did he have before he gave away part of his collection?

13. Tony buys a binder for $17.25 and a pen for $2.75. He pays $\frac{7}{100}$ of the total price in taxes. How much did he pay in taxes?

14. Blanca spends $500.00 on furniture. She spends $\frac{3}{10}$ of the money on a chair, $50.00 on a table, and the rest on a sofa.

What fraction of the $500.00 did she spend on each item?

15. A leap year happens every 4 years. How many times will a leap year happen in 60 years?

16. The heart pumps about $\frac{1}{16}$ L of blood with each beat. About how many times would the heart need to beat to pump 4 L of blood?

17. The price of a movie ticket is $7.00 now. If the price rises by $0.15 each year, how much will the ticket cost in 10 years?

18. A cup of raspberries weighs about 7 ounces. A recipe calls for $2\frac{1}{4}$ cups of raspberries. About how many ounces of raspberries are needed?

# 54. Order of Operations and Brackets

Add and subtract in the order you read: from left to right.

1. Add or subtract from left to right.

   a) $5 + 4 - 3$

      $= 9 - 3$

      $= 6$

   b) $6 - 4 + 1$

   c) $4 + 5 + 3$

   d) $9 - 3 - 2$

Multiply and divide in the order you read: from left to right.

2. Multiply or divide from left to right.

   a) $3 \times 4 \div 2$

      $= 12 \div 2$

      $= 6$

   b) $6 \div 3 \times 2$

   c) $7 \times 3 \times 2$

   d) $12 \div 3 \div 2$

When doing operations…

**Step 1:** Do all multiplications and divisions from left to right.

**Step 2:** Do all additions and subtractions from left to right.

3. Circle the operation you would do first.

   a) $5 + (2 \times 3)$

   b) $9 - 2 + 5$

   c) $10 + 5 \div 5$

   d) $11 - 8 \div 2$

   e) $12 \div 3 \times 2$

   f) $10 - 3 \times 3$

   g) $8 + 2 - 5$

   h) $5 \times 5 - 6$

   i) $18 \div 6 + 3$

   j) $15 \div 5 - 2$

   k) $2 \times 3 + 4$

   l) $4 \times 6 \div 2$

4. Circle and do the first operation. Then rewrite the rest of the expression.

   a) $(5 + 8) - 4$

      $= \underline{\quad 13 - 4 \quad}$

   b) $5 + (6 \div 3)$

      $= \underline{\quad 5 + 2 \quad}$

   c) $12 \div 4 + 2$

      $= \underline{\qquad\qquad}$

   d) $18 \div 6 \times 3$

      $= \underline{\qquad\qquad}$

   e) $10 - 5 - 3$

      $= \underline{\qquad\qquad}$

   f) $2 \times 6 \div 3$

      $= \underline{\qquad\qquad}$

   g) $16 \div 4 - 3$

      $= \underline{\qquad\qquad}$

   h) $11 - 5 + 5$

      $= \underline{\qquad\qquad}$

   i) $2 \times 30 \div 20$

      $= \underline{\qquad\qquad}$

   j) $7 \times 4 - 3$

      $= \underline{\qquad\qquad}$

   k) $36 \div 4 + 3$

      $= \underline{\qquad\qquad}$

   l) $20 - 5 \times 3$

      $= \underline{\qquad\qquad}$

Brackets change the order of operations. Do the operations in brackets before all others.

Example: $7 - 3 + 2 = 4 + 2$    but    $7 - (3 + 2) = 7 - 5$
$\qquad\qquad\qquad = 6 \qquad\qquad\qquad\qquad\qquad\qquad = 2$

**5.** Do the operation in brackets first. Then write the answer.

a) $(7 + 3) \times 2$

$= 10 \times 2$

$= 20$

b) $7 + (3 \times 2)$

c) $(7 + 3) \div 2$

d) $(7 - 3) \div 2$

e) $7 - (3 \times 2)$

f) $(7 - 3) \times 2$

g) $2 + (3 - 1)$

h) $8 - (6 \div 3)$

i) $4 \times (2 \times 3)$

j) $(4 \times 2) \times 3$

k) $(12 \div 6) \div 2$

l) $12 \div (6 \div 2)$

**6.** a) Add the same numbers in two ways. Do the addition in brackets first.

i) $(2 + 3) + 8$ $\qquad$ $2 + (3 + 8)$

$= \underline{\quad} + 8$ $\qquad$ $= 2 + \underline{\quad}$

$= \underline{\quad}$ $\qquad\qquad$ $= \underline{\quad}$

ii) $(5 + 2) + 4$ $\qquad$ $5 + (2 + 4)$

$= \underline{\quad} + \underline{\quad}$ $\qquad$ $= \underline{\quad} + \underline{\quad}$

$= \underline{\quad}$ $\qquad\qquad$ $= \underline{\quad}$

b) Does the answer change depending on which addition you do first? _____

**7.** a) Subtract the same numbers in two ways. Do the subtraction in brackets first.

i) $(9 - 5) - 2$ $\qquad$ $9 - (5 - 2)$

$= \underline{\quad} - \underline{\quad}$ $\qquad$ $= \underline{\quad} - \underline{\quad}$

$= \underline{\quad}$ $\qquad\qquad$ $= \underline{\quad}$

ii) $11 - (6 - 5)$ $\qquad$ $(11 - 6) - 5$

$= \underline{\quad} - \underline{\quad}$ $\qquad$ $= \underline{\quad} - \underline{\quad}$

$= \underline{\quad}$ $\qquad\qquad$ $= \underline{\quad}$

b) Does the answer change depending on which subtraction you do first? _____

# 55. Numerical Expressions

A **numerical expression** is a combination of numbers, operation signs, and sometimes brackets that represents a quantity.

Example: These numerical expressions all represent 10.

$5 + 2 + 3$ $\qquad\qquad$ $14 - 4$ $\qquad\qquad$ $70 \div 7$ $\qquad\qquad$ $(3 + 2) \times 2$

1. Calculate the numerical expression by considering the order of operations.

a) $2 + 5 + 1$ _____

b) $2 \times 5$ _____

c) $3 \times 2 \times 1$ _____

d) $3 + 4 \times 1$ _____

e) $3 + 4 \div 2$ _____

f) $8 \times 3 \div 2$ _____

g) $(1 + 3) \times 4$ _____

h) $3 + (6 \div 2)$ _____

i) $(6 \times 3) \div 2$ _____

j) $(10 - 4) \div 2$ _____

k) $10 - (4 \div 2)$ _____

l) $5 \times (3 \times 2)$ _____

2. Write the number 3 in the box and then calculate the expression.

a) $\boxed{3} + 4 \longrightarrow \underline{\ 7\ }$

b) $\boxed{3} + 2 \longrightarrow$ _____

c) $\boxed{\phantom{3}} + 5 \longrightarrow$ _____

d) $9 - \boxed{\phantom{3}} \longrightarrow$ _____

e) $17 - \boxed{\phantom{3}} \longrightarrow$ _____

f) $\boxed{\phantom{3}} - 2 \longrightarrow$ _____

g) $2 \times \boxed{\phantom{3}} \longrightarrow$ _____

h) $\boxed{\phantom{3}} \times 5 \longrightarrow$ _____

i) $3 \times \boxed{\phantom{3}} \longrightarrow$ _____

j) $6 \div \boxed{\phantom{3}} \longrightarrow$ _____

k) $15 \div \boxed{\phantom{3}} \longrightarrow$ _____

l) $\boxed{\phantom{3}} \div 3 \longrightarrow$ _____

*Any* number can be in an expression—not just whole numbers.

Examples:

$2.7 + 4.1$ $\qquad\qquad$ $\dfrac{4}{5} - \dfrac{1}{5}$ $\qquad\qquad$ $(2 + 3) \div \dfrac{1}{4}$

3. Calculate the numerical expression.

a) $2.3 + 1.6$ _____

b) $3 \times 2.1$ _____

c) $2 \times 3.2$ _____

d) $\dfrac{2}{5} + \dfrac{1}{5}$ _____

e) $2 \div \dfrac{1}{3}$ _____

f) $3 \times \dfrac{2}{7}$ _____

g) $\left(\dfrac{1}{7} + \dfrac{3}{7}\right) \times 2$ _____

h) $5 + (4 \times 1.2)$ _____

BONUS ▶ $\left(\dfrac{1}{5} \times \dfrac{3}{4}\right) \times 2$ _____

An **equation** is a statement that has two equal expressions separated by an equal sign.

Examples: $14 - 4 = 70 \div 7$    $12 = 3 \times 4$

4.  a)  Circle two expressions in Question 1 that represent the same number.

    b)  Write an equation using the two expressions.

    _____ = _____

5.  Verify that the equation is true.

    a)  $(4 + 3) \times 2 = (5 \times 3) - 1$

    $(4 + 3) \times 2$  and  $(5 \times 3) - 1$

    $= 7 \times 2$        $= 15 - 1$

    $= 14$              $= 14$

    b)  $2 \times 4 \times 5 = 4 \times 10$

    $2 \times 4 \times 5$  and  $4 \times 10$

    c)  $3 + 11 = (3 + 1) + (11 - 1)$
    $3 + 11$  and  $(3 + 1) + (11 - 1)$

    d)  $3 + 11 = (3 + 2) + (11 - 2)$
    $3 + 11$  and  $(3 + 2) + (11 - 2)$

6.  Peter calculated $12 - 4 \times 2$ and got 16. What mistake did he make? Explain.

    _____

    _____

**BONUS** ▶ Add brackets to show which operation was done first.

    a)  $8 - 3 \times 2 = 10$

    b)  $11 - 3 \times 3 = 2$

    c)  $7 \times 3 - 2 = 7$

    d)  $12 \div 3 \times 2 = 2$

    e)  $6 - 2 \times 3 = 0$

    f)  $3 \times 6 \div 2 = 9$

# 56. Unknown Quantities and Equations

1. Some apples are inside a bag and some are outside the bag. The total number of apples is shown. Draw the missing apples in the bag.

a) 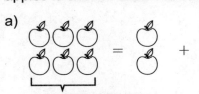 = 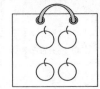 + 

total number of apples

b)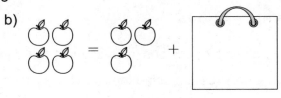

c) 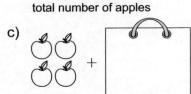 + 

d)

2. Draw the missing apples in the bag. Then write an equation (with numbers) to represent the picture.

a)

_5_ = _3_ + ☐

b)

____ = ____ + ☐

c)

____ + ☐ = ____

d)

____ + ☐ = ____

3. Write an equation for each problem. Use a box for the unknown quantity.

a) There are 7 apples altogether. There are 4 outside a basket. How many are inside?

_7_ = _4_ + ☐

b) There are 9 apples altogether. There are 7 outside a basket. How many are inside?

____ = ____ + ☐

c) There are 11 plums altogether. There are 5 inside a bag. How many are outside?

d) 17 students are at the library. There are 9 in the computer room. How many are outside the computer room?

4. Jeff took some apples from a bag. Show how many apples were in the bag originally.

a) 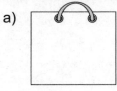 −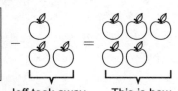

Jeff took away this many.  This is how many were left.

b)  −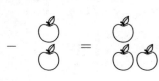

**5.** Show how many apples were in the bag originally. Then write an equation to represent the picture.

a)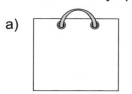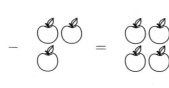

$$\boxed{\phantom{0}} - 3 = 4$$

b)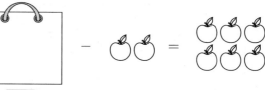

$$\boxed{\phantom{0}} - 2 = 6$$

**6.** Find the number that makes the equation true and write it in the box.

a) $\boxed{6} + 3 = 9$

b) $\boxed{\phantom{0}} + 4 = 9$

c) $\boxed{\phantom{0}} + 5 = 9$

d) $8 - \boxed{\phantom{0}} = 5$

e) $13 - \boxed{\phantom{0}} = 11$

f) $19 - \boxed{\phantom{0}} = 8$

g) $3 \times \boxed{\phantom{0}} = 6$

h) $4 \times \boxed{\phantom{0}} = 20$

i) $2 \times \boxed{\phantom{0}} = 2$

j) $\boxed{\phantom{0}} \div 3 = 5$

k) $\boxed{\phantom{0}} \div 5 = 3$

l) $\boxed{\phantom{0}} \div 13 = 1$

m) $3 + 6 = 5 + \boxed{\phantom{0}}$

n) $10 - 3 = \boxed{\phantom{0}} + 4$

o) $1 + 5 = 7 - \boxed{\phantom{0}}$

**BONUS ▶** Put the same number in both boxes to make each equation true.

p) $\boxed{\phantom{0}} + 3 = 11 - \boxed{\phantom{0}}$

q) $\boxed{\phantom{0}} \div 2 = \boxed{\phantom{0}} - 2$

r) $\boxed{\phantom{0}} \times \boxed{\phantom{0}} = 16$

**7.** Find the missing number for the problem and write it in the box.

a) There are 10 marbles. / 4 are outside the box. / How many are inside?

$$10 = 4 + \boxed{\phantom{0}}$$

b) There are 9 cards. / 6 are outside the box. / How many are inside?

$$9 = 6 + \boxed{\phantom{0}}$$

c) There are 12 children in a class. / 7 are girls. / How many are boys?

$$12 = 7 + \boxed{\phantom{0}}$$

d) A cat had 7 kittens. / 4 kittens are striped. / How many are not striped?

$$7 = 4 + \boxed{\phantom{0}}$$

e) Paul had some stickers. / He gave away 3. / 4 were left.

$$\boxed{\phantom{0}} - 3 = 4$$

f) There are 15 oranges in boxes. / How many oranges are in each box? / There are 3 boxes.

$$15 \div \boxed{\phantom{0}} = 3$$

# 57. Translating Words into Expressions

1. Match the description with the correct numerical expression.

   2 more than 6         $4 \times 6$       2 divided into 11     $3 \times 11$

   6 divided by 3        $6 - 2$       11 reduced by 4     $11 \div 2$

   2 less than 6         $6 + 2$       11 times 3         $11 + 3$

   the product of 6 and 4    $6 - 3$       twice as many as 11    $11 - 4$

   6 decreased by 3      $6 \div 3$       11 increased by 3    $2 \times 11$

2. Write an expression for each description.

   a) 4 more than 3   _$3 + 4$_          b) 15 decreased by 8.5 _____

   c) 24 divided by 8 _____         d) 2 less than 9   _$9 - 2$_

   e) 6.7 increased by 2.9 _____    f) 3.5 added to 4 _____

   g) twice as many as 5 _____      h) 12 divided by 5 _____

   i) the product of 7 and $\dfrac{2}{3}$ _____    j) 5 times $\dfrac{1}{3}$ _____

3. Turn the written instructions into mathematical expressions.

   a) Add 8 and 3.   _$8 + 3$_       b) Divide 6 by 2. _____

   c) Add 3.4 and 9. _____        d) Subtract 5 from 7. _____

   e) Multiply 4.2 and 2. _____     f) Decrease 3 by $\dfrac{2}{5}$. _____

   g) Add 8 and 4. Then divide by 3. _____

   h) Divide 8 by 4. Then add 5. _____

   i) Divide 4 by 2. Then add 10. Then subtract 4. _____

   j) Multiply 6 and 5. Then subtract 20. Then divide by 2. _____

4. Write the mathematical expressions in words.

   a) $(6 + 2) \times 3$   _Add 6 and 2. Then multiply by 3._

   b) $(6 + 1) \times 2$ _____

   c) $12 - 5 \times 2$ _____

   d) $(3 - 2) \times 4$ _____

   e) $4 \times (3 - 1 + 5)$ _____

5. How far will a motorcycle travel at the speed and in the time given? Write the numerical expression.

   a) Speed: 60 miles per hour
      Time: 2 hours

      Distance: ___60 × 2___ miles

   b) Speed: 80 km per hour
      Time: 4 hours

      Distance: _____ km

   c) Speed: 70 km per hour
      Time: 5 hours

      Distance: _____ km

6. a) How much will it cost to rent a bike for the time given? Write the numerical expression.

      i)  1 hour: _____5 × 1_____     ii)  2 hours: _____     iii)  4 hours: _____

   b) Complete to explain the expression.

      i)   5 × 3 is the cost of renting a bike for __3__ hours.

      ii)  5 × 2 is the cost of renting a bike for ____ hours.

      iii) 5 × 5 is the cost of renting a bike for ____ hours.

      RENT A BIKE
      $5 an hour

7. a) A different rental company charges $6 per bike and then $3 for each hour.
      Write the numerical expression for the cost of renting a bike for…

      i)  1 hour: ____6 + 3 × 1____     ii)  2 hours: _____     iii)  4 hours: _____

   b) Complete the description of each expression.

      i)   6 + 3 × 3 is the cost of renting a bike for __3__ hours.

      ii)  6 + 3 × 2 is the cost of renting a bike for ____ hours.

      iii) 6 + 3 × 5 is the cost of renting a bike for ____ hours.

8. A field trip for a Grade 5 class costs $11 per student plus $2 for a snack.

   a) Write an expression to represent the cost for 1 student and 1 snack.    _____

   b) Write an expression to represent the cost for 3 students and 3 snacks.    _____

   BONUS ▶ Write a word problem that could be represented by 19 × (11 + 2).

9. A day pass can be used by 2 adults and 2 children for unlimited one-day bus travel
   on weekends. Write an expression to represent the number of day passes that are
   needed for 10 adults and 10 children.

10. 20 students from each class go to the museum. There are 5 classes, along with
    13 teachers and 16 parents.

    a) Write an expression to represent the number of people that go to the museum.

    b) How many buses will be needed if 30 people ride in each bus?

## 58. Tape Diagrams I

Maria has 7 music albums. Clara has 3 times as many albums as Maria does. Maria uses a **tape diagram** to find out the number of albums Clara has.

Maria's albums: | 7 |

Clara's albums: | 7 | 7 | 7 | ← Clara has $3 \times 7 = 21$ albums.

A tape diagram has two strips on top of each other with the same unit, but different sizes.

1. Draw a tape diagram to model the story.

   a) Clara has 3 stickers. Yu has 4 times as many stickers as Clara does.

   Clara's stickers: | 3 |

   Yu's stickers: | 3 | 3 | 3 | 3 |

   b) There are 7 blue balloons. There are 3 times as many red balloons.

   _____

   _____

   c) There are 8 red apples. There are 4 times as many green apples as red apples.

   d) Blanca has 4 books. Mia has 5 times as many books.

You can use a tape diagram to find out the total number of something. Example:

Maria's albums: | 7 |

Clara's albums: | 7 | 7 | 7 | } ← $7 + 21$
There are 28 albums in total.

2. Solve the problem by drawing a tape diagram.

   a) Jin has 5 cards. Rob has 3 times as many cards as Jin. How many cards do they have together?

   Jin's cards: 5 | 5 |

   Rob's cards: 15 | 5 | 5 | 5 |

   _5_ + _15_ = _20_ , so Jin and Rob have _20_ cards together.

   b) Luis studies toads and frogs. He has 6 toads and twice as many frogs. How many animals does he have altogether?

   Toads: _____

   Frogs: _____

   _____ + _____ = _____ , so Luis has _____ animals altogether.

**c)** There are 24 round crackers in a box. There are 4 times as many square crackers in the box. How many crackers are there altogether?

**d)** There are 13 biographies in a school library. There are 3 times as many fiction books in the library. How many biographies and fiction books are in the library altogether?

3. Draw a tape diagram for the story. Then write the given number beside the correct bar.

a) There are 20 oranges. There are 4 times as many oranges as apples.

Oranges: 20 [ ][ ][ ][ ]

Apples: _____ [ ]

b) There are 35 grandparents in the audience. There are 7 times as many grandparents as kids.

_____

_____

**c)** Layi spent $31.50 on her shoes and three times as much on her pants.

**d)** Grace studied math for 45 minutes and science for twice as much time.

4. All the blocks in each problem are the same size. What is the size of 1 block?

a)

| 6 | 6 | 6 | 6 |

| 6 | 18 |

b)

[ ][ ][ ][ ]

[ ][ ] 18

c)

[ ][ ][ ]
[ ]

total: 20

d)

[ ][ ][ ][ ]
[ ][ ]

total: 42

5. Show on the tape diagram what represents 12 beads. What is the size of 1 block?

a) There are 12 red beads.

green | 2 |

red | 2 | 2 | 2 | 2 | 2 | 2 |

12

b) There are 12 beads in total.

green [ ]

red [ ][ ][ ]

c) There are 12 more red beads than green.

green [ ][ ][ ]

red [ ][ ][ ][ ][ ]

d) There are 12 green beads.

green [ ][ ][ ]

red [ ][ ]

# 59. Tape Diagrams II

1. The bars below represent the number of green (g) and red (r) beads in a box.
   Fill in the blanks.

   a) g: ▢▢          4 more red beads than green beads

   r: ▢▢▢          1 block = _____ beads, so _____ beads in total

   b) g: ▢▢▢        12 beads altogether

   r: ▢             1 block = _____ , so _____ green beads

   c) g: ▢▢▢        10 more red beads than green beads

   r: ▢▢▢▢▢        1 block = _____ beads, so _____ beads in total

   d) g: ▢▢          35 beads altogether

   r: ▢▢▢▢          1 block = _____ , so _____ green beads

2. Use the tape diagram to find the number of red and green beads.

   a) $\frac{2}{3}$ as many green beads as red beads

   10 more red beads than green beads

   g: ▢▢

   r: ▢▢▢

   red: _____   green: _____

   b) $\frac{3}{7}$ as many red beads as green beads.

   30 beads altogether

   r: ▢▢▢

   g: ▢▢▢▢▢▢▢

   red: _____   green: _____

   c) $\frac{1}{4}$ as many green beads as red beads

   12 more red beads than green beads

   g: ▢

   r: ▢▢▢▢

   red: _____   green: _____

   d) $\frac{2}{5}$ as many red beads as green beads.

   35 beads altogether

   r: ▢▢

   g: ▢▢▢▢▢

   red: _____   green: _____

3. Draw a tape diagram for the problem. Find the length of 1 block. Then solve the problem.

a) Jay has 3 times as many cards as Omar. Jay has 12 more cards than Omar. How many cards does each boy have?

| Jay's cards | 6 | 6 | 6 |
| Omar's cards | 6 | 12 | |

Jay has __18__ cards, and Omar has __6__ cards.

b) Mike is 3 times as old as Kim. Mike is 14 years older than Kim. How old are Mike and Kim?

__Kim__

__Mike__

Mike is ___ years old, and Kim is ___ years old.

c) There are 6 times as many balloons as flags to decorate the house. There are 35 decorations altogether. How many balloons and how many flags are there?

There are _____ balloons and _____ flags.

d) To make 2 cups of boiled rice, you need 2 cups of water and 1 cup of dry rice. Anna wants to cook 4 cups of boiled rice. How much water and how much dry rice does she need?

Anna needs _____ cups of water and

_____ cups of dry rice.

4. Draw a model to answer the question.

Sara walks 4 times as far to school as Borana. Sara walks 6 more blocks than Borana. How many blocks do they each walk?

Sara:

Borana:

Sara: _____      Borana: _____

5. A pair of shoes costs twice as much as a T-shirt. George paid $34.50 for a pair of shoes and a T-shirt. How much does each item cost?

_____

_____

**BONUS ▶** How much would George pay for three pairs of shoes and two T-shirts?

# 60. Variables

1. You can rent skates for $3 an hour. Write a numerical expression for the cost of renting skates for...

   a) 2 hours: _3 × 2_          b) 5 hours: _____          c) 6 hours: _____

---

A **variable** is a letter or symbol (such as *w*, *T*, or *h*) that represents a number.

To make an **algebraic expression**, replace some numbers in a numerical expression with variables.

Examples of algebraic expressions:     $w + 1$          $3 + 4 \times T$          $2 + t - 3 \times h$

---

2. Write an expression for the distance a car would travel at the speed and in the time given.

   a) Speed: 60 km per hour       b) Speed: 50 miles per hour       c) Speed: 70 km per hour

   Time: 3 hours                  Time: 4 hours                     Time: *h* hours

   Distance: _____ km        Distance: _____ miles        Distance: _____ km

---

In the product of a number and a variable, the multiplication sign is usually dropped.

   $3 \times T$ can be written as $3T$   and   $5 \times z$ can be written as $5z$.

---

3. Renting skis costs $5 an hour. Write a numerical expression for the cost of renting skis for...

   a) *h* hours: _5 × h_ or _5h_       b) *t* hours: _____ or _____

   c) *x* hours: _____ or _____    d) *n* hours: _____ or _____

---

When replacing a variable with a number, use brackets.

Example: Replacing *n* with 7 in the expression $3n$ gives $3(7)$, which is another way to write $3 \times 7$.

---

4. Write the number 2 in the brackets and evaluate.

   a) $5(2) =$ _5 × 2_ = _10_       b) $3(\quad) =$ _____ = ____       c) $4(\quad) =$ _____ = ____

   d) $2(\quad) + 5$               e) $4(\quad) - 2$                     f) $6(\quad) + 3$

5. Replace the variable with the given number and then evaluate.

   a) $2h + 5$,  $h = 3$           b) $3n + 2$,  $n = 5$                 c) $4t - 1$,  $t = 2$

   $2(3) + 5$

   $= 6 + 5$

   $= 11$

   d) $2m + 7$,  $m = 6$           e) $8 - 2z$,  $z = 3$                 f) $7n - 6$,  $n = 4$

---

**JUMP Math Accumula**

# 61. Multiplication and Word Problems

There are 4 times as many cats as dogs.

$4 > 1$, so there are more cats than dogs.

The number of cats is the *larger* quantity (L).
The number of dogs is the *smaller* quantity (S).

There are $\frac{1}{3}$ as many pears as bananas.

$\frac{1}{3} < 1$, so there are more bananas than pears.

The number of bananas is the *larger* quantity (L).
The number of pears is the *smaller* quantity (S).

1. Fill in the table.

|  |  | Larger Quantity (L) | Smaller Quantity (S) |
|---|---|---|---|
| a) | There are 4 times as many plums as apples. | *plums* | *apples* |
| b) | There are 3 times as many dogs as cats. |  |  |
| c) | There are $\frac{1}{4}$ as many eggs as nests. |  |  |
| d) | There are half as many boys as girls. |  |  |
| e) | Ron is twice as old as Maria. | *Ron's age* |  |
| f) | A cat is $\frac{1}{5}$ as heavy as a dog. |  |  |

The **scale factor** is a number you multiply a quantity or a length by to change size.

If the scale factor is greater than 1,
$L = $ scale factor $\times S$.

Example: $L = 4 \times S$

If the scale factor is smaller than 1,
$S = $ scale factor $\times L$.

Example: $S = \frac{1}{3} \times L$

2. *L* is the larger quantity and *S* is the smaller quantity. Circle the correct equations.

$L = 4 \times S$       $S = 4 \times L$       $L = \frac{1}{5} \times S$       $S = \frac{1}{3} \times L$       $L = 2.5 \times S$

3. Write *L* above the larger quantity and *S* above the smaller quantity. Then write the equation.

     L                        S
a) A book is 3 times as heavy as a notebook.        $L = 3 \times S$

b) A shelf is 3 times as tall as a stool.        _____

c) My cat is half as heavy as my dog.        _____

d) Alicia is twice as old as Yu.        _____

e) There are $\frac{1}{5}$ as many mice as hamsters in a pet store.   _____

4. Write *L* above the larger quantity and *S* above the smaller quantity everywhere. Write the equation. Then replace the correct letter with the given number.

a) 
$$\overset{L}{\text{A book}}\text{ is 4 times as heavy as a }\overset{S}{\text{notebook}}.$$

The book weighs 400 g.

$$\underline{L = 4 \times S}$$

$$\underline{400 = 4 \times S}$$

b) There are 3 times as many pears as apples.

There are 12 apples.

_____

_____

c) Ava is half as old as Ken.

Ken is 6 years old.

_____

_____

d) A tree is 6 times as tall as a bush.

The tree is 18 m tall.

_____

_____

e) Mona has $\frac{1}{5}$ as much money as Leo.
Leo has $10.

_____

_____

f) A break is $\frac{1}{6}$ as long as a lesson.
The break lasts 15 minutes.

_____

_____

---

The equations $L = 4 \times S$ and $S = \frac{1}{4} \times L$ mean the same thing.

---

5. Write the equation that means the same thing.

a) $L = 2 \times S$

$S = \frac{1}{2} \times L$

_____

b) $S = \frac{1}{5} \times L$

_____

c) $L = 6 \times S$

_____

d) $S = \frac{1}{3} \times L$

_____

6. Write the equation and replace the correct letter with the given number.
If the unknown is not by itself, write the equation that means the same thing.
Solve the equation to solve the problem.

a) There are 3 times as many cats as dogs in a shelter. There are 12 cats in the shelter. How many dogs are there?

b) Nina is half as old as Jose. Jose is 12. How old is Nina?

c) A snake is 5 times as long as a lizard. The snake is 125 cm long. How long is the lizard?

d) A scarf costs $\frac{1}{3}$ as much as a hat. The scarf costs $8. How much does the hat cost?